Marci Baker's

Oh My Stars!

**STRIP-PIECED –
REALLY!**

Alicia's Attic
Fort Collins, Colorado
www.aliciasattic.com

Clearview Triangle

©2009, Marci Baker
Editor: Marci Baker
Assistant Editor: Anita Hartinger
Assistant Editor: Alicia Sanchez
Production Coordinator: Susan Simono
Graphic Design & Layout: Mark Talbot of Xplore Design, Inc.
www.xplore-design.com
Cover Design: Marci Baker/Mark Talbot
Photography: Randy Pfizenmaier of Fusebox Studios, except as noted
www.fuseboxstudio.com
Printing: Cedar Graphics, Hiawatha, IA
www.cedargraphicsinc.com

Published by Alicia's Attic, Inc., Fort Collins, CO
1-888-348-6653, 970-224-1336, fax 970-224-1362
www.aliciasattic.com, info@aliciasattic.com

Printed in the United States of America
ISBN: 0-9651439-5-3
Library of Congress Control Number: 2009903839

On the front cover:
Center - "City Lights" by Scott Hansen
Left - "Galaxy of Stars" by Marci Baker
Right - "All Stars" by Marci Baker

On the back cover:
"All Stars" by Nanette Dailey (Quilted by Patti Heintz)
"Carolina Lily" by Bobbie Crosby
"Galaxy of Stars" by Marci Baker
"My Sister's Tote" by Marci Baker
"Stars & Stripes" by Anita Hartinger

Acknowledgements

Long awaited, here is the stars technique replayed with a wide variety of designs. With God's blessings, this exploration of stars has coalesced from the talents of many contributors.

Thank you to Kerry Cain and Shirley Gisi for sharing your creations. Thank you to Elisheva Salamo for giving me the opportunity to design the challah cover. Your designs have added robustness to the book.

To Leoba ("Lee") Weishaar, thank you for your patience and diligence and for sharing your hero's quilt with all of us – a truly heartwarming story.

Thank you to Janice Schlieker for inspiring and for creating several designs. Also, thank you to Brenda Backx, Nanette Daily, Mary Harpold, and Jenny Hubbard for providing different variations of the quilts.

To Bobbie Crosby, thank you for taking on several projects and going a step further with the Carolina Lily table runner.

To Scott Hansen, thank you for stepping outside your quilting box and making the City Lights in such a short time. Excellent interpretation!

Thank you to Heather Carruthers, Margaret Dart, Wendy Klein, Elaine Muzichuk, Joy Schneider, Linda Seemann-Korte, and Marj Tyess for testing the rough draft and for giving feedback on ways to improve the instructions.

Thank you to Jan and Jay Bowser for teaching and allowing me to use your Gammill longarm. The late nights to meet the deadline were above and beyond the call – photography happened as needed because of your devotion and flexibility.

Thank you to Susan Simono for being the main contact for our external support personnel. Thank you to Anita Hartinger for your dedication and inspiring ideas for several projects. Also, thanks to Alicia Sanchez for working through my engineering style and for being a tester of pre-rough-draft materials.

Thank you to Mark Talbot and Randy Pfizenmaier for another job well done and a great working relationship. You guys are the best!

Thank you to my family who has understood when I said, "I'm working on the book again tonight," for many, many nights.

Lastly, thank you to my students over the years who have taught me so much. I will continue to develop and teach even more frustration-free quilting as long as you are there.

With special thanks to these professional entities for supporting the art and craft of quilting:
Collections from Lecien, www.lecien.co.jp/en
Michael Miller Fabrics LLC, www.michaelmillerfabrics.com
Moda Fabrics, www.modafabrics.com
Northcott Fabrics, www.northcott.com
P&B Textiles, www.pbtex.com
Presencia USA, www.threads.com
Quilter's Dream Batting, www.quiltersbatting.com
Rowan and FreeSpirit fabric by Westminster Fibers Lifestyle Fabrics, www.freespiritfabric.com
National Museum of American History, Smithsonian Institute, www.americanhistory.si.edu
Tennessee Quilts
Windham Fabrics, www.windhamfabrics.com

Dedication

To Sara and Dale Nephew for supporting me in reaching the stars!
Thank you for your trust and for believing in me.

To FSQ6,

Enjoy!

Marci L Baker

Table of Contents

Original drawing used by permission of Steven Renshaw and Saori Ihara, adapted by Mark Talbot

The Attraction of Stars

The beauty and intrigue of star patterns is universal. You will find the usage of star designs in all cultures. The six-pointed star has a special distinction throughout history by its use in art and architecture across the globe. As discovered by historians and archeologists, stars were used abundantly on fretwork, friezes, paintings, and manuscripts. Down through the ages to today, its use is evident in many cultures, such as in Arabian rose-work, Byzantine mosaics, and Eastern Indian art, as decorative and practical motifs.

In Japanese lore, the study of stars literally affected cultural lifestyle. The four outer stars within the Orion constellation, were viewed as a woman's kimono sleeve gracefully draping toward the Southern Sky. These stars also represented points of history, seasonal markers for planting crops, or times when the best fishing would occur.

Representations, meanings, and symbolizations of stars are as infinite as the universe. How ever they are viewed, stars are used in many ways, shapes, and forms around the globe. As proven by earth's history, we are all attracted to stars no matter what walk of life, culture, or belief drives our existence.

Behind the Gas and Dust of Orion's Trapezium Cluster
Photo Courtesy NASA and STScI
http://hubblesite.org

Stars…Strip-Pieced - REALLY!

In our heritage of quilting, the six-pointed star is usually constructed with inset seams. Therefore designs have only been completed effectively by the most accomplished of quilters, until now.

From a simple single-fabric star to multi-fabric scrappy stars, the process is as easy as sewing strips together in straight seams! No insets! No Y-seams! Here's how…

If you understand how a star is formed (not the ones in the night sky but the ones of fabric), you'll better visualize why each step is needed. I have found, even in quilting, that it is easier to get somewhere if you have a basic concept of how and where you are going. Look at the photo. Do you see blocks? (Look where only three fabrics touch.) Can you see stars? (Look where six fabrics come together.) Both blocks and stars are made using 60-degree diamonds. We are aiming for stars. We'll be selecting fabrics and sewing them together to get six diamonds of "similar" value surrounded by diamonds of a high contrast background fabric. This shape is the basis for all of the designs shown in this book.

This fabric was pieced for a kimono using Lecien fabrics. The subtle value differences make the star and block shapes shimmer across the garment. The strong star design effectively shows the high contrast required to make the stars stand out on the sleeves and back yoke.

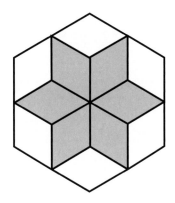

As mentioned earlier, blocks can be seen in the star design. It turns out that each star is three blocks, A, B, and C. Notice that within each block the position of the background diamond (the lighter diamond) matches the location of the block in the star. For A, the background diamond is at the top of the block so A is the top of the star. For B, the background diamond is on the left so B is the leftside of the star. For C, the background diamond is on the right so C is the right side of the star. Remembering this will help with layout later on.

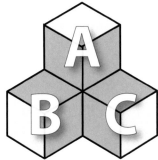

You may be thinking that this is all fine and dandy, but you still see set-in seams. The uniqueness of this method is that each block is made up of two half-blocks, left and right, which makes a seam through the top diamond.

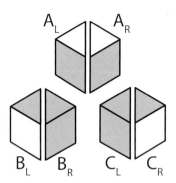

To save time and effort, the left and right half-blocks are cut from strip-sets that are sewn with varying combinations of background and star fabrics. After laying out the shapes into stars, they are sewn together, one above the other, into long strips such that when the strips are sewn together, the stars appear.

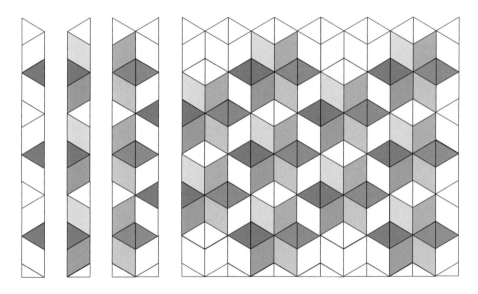

Each project gives detailed instructions of what to cut and sew to make these pieces. Here are terms and sample diagrams used throughout the book:

Strip-Set:	Three strips are sewn together, pressed, then cut into left or right half-blocks.
Star Set:	The six strip-sets (sometimes only three) needed to cut the different half-blocks required for a star.
Half-Block:	The shape, either left or right, cut from the strip-sets.
FW:	A strip cut to the full width of the fabric – at least 40" long.
1/2W:	" half-width of fabric – at least 20" long.
1/3W:	" third-width of fabric – at least 13" long.
1/4W:	" quarter-width of fabric – at least 10" long.
1/8W:	" eighth-width of fabric – at least 5" long.

Star Set Diagram:

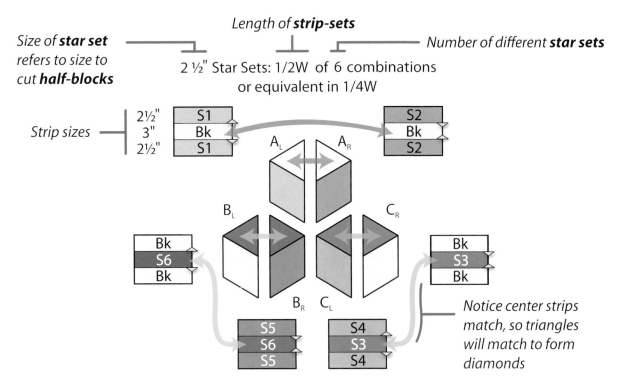

Length of **strip-sets**

Size of **star set** refers to size to cut **half-blocks**

Number of different **star sets**

2 ½" Star Sets: 1/2W of 6 combinations
or equivalent in 1/4W

Strip sizes

2½"
3"
2½"

S1
Bk
S1

S2
Bk
S2

A_L A_R

B_L C_R

Bk
S6
Bk

Bk
S3
Bk

B_R C_L

S5
S6
S5

S4
S3
S4

Notice center strips match, so triangles will match to form diamonds

Cut Half-Blocks Diagram:

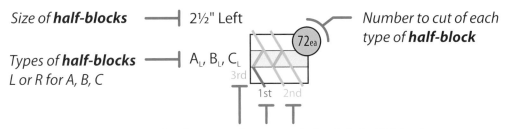

Size of **half-blocks** — 2½" Left

Number to cut of each type of **half-block**

72ea

Types of **half-blocks** L or R for A, B, C

A_L, B_L, C_L

3rd

1st 2nd

A visual reference of **cuts** made for **left half-blocks**
See page 108 for full details

Cut Shapes Diagram:

Size and Shape to cut — 2¾" Half-Triangles

Types of **fabric: number of strips**

Bk: 4⁺ Strips
2½" x 1/4W

34

1st 2nd 3rd

Number to cut

Width and length of strips

A visual reference of **cuts** made for the **shape**
See page 114 for full details

Layout Diagram:

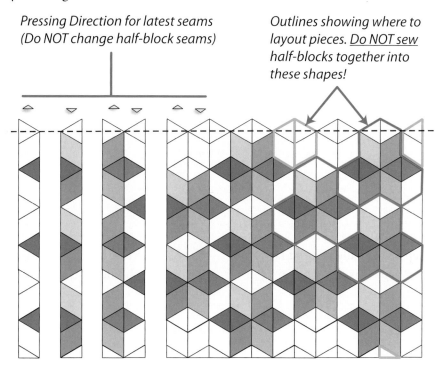

Pressing Direction for latest seams (Do NOT change half-block seams)

Outlines showing where to layout pieces. Do NOT sew half-blocks together into these shapes!

Throughout the book you will find tips for all levels of quilters. We have defined them as follows:

New Quilter? For the quilter wanting help at critical steps.

Want a Tip? For confident quilters wanting a little extra information in the process.

Designing Quilter? For the quilter wanting a change and ready for a challenge.

With this brief overview, we have a basic concept of the formation of stars. In the next sections we will cover fabric selection, tools, and other basic requirements. Then you can select from the variety of designs provided and begin your own star creation. If you are ever "lost" come back to this overview to see how the step you are working on fits into the overall picture.

Know Before You Sew

Choose Your Fabric

As seen in the last section, the values of the fabric chosen will make a big difference in the finished effect. In order to make the stars stand out, select fabrics such that any star fabrics are relatively close to each other in value when compared to the background. In some cases you may want to fade the stars as was done in Galaxy of Stars, page 53. This was accomplished by choosing the star fabrics to get closer and closer in value to the background fabric.

When making your choices, you can use any type of print, stripe, or plaid except diagonally printed fabrics. Diagonal prints create an obvious discord when placed as the top diamond in a block. Prints should read as an overall value or be in high contrast to the background. Too large of print with both light and dark sections can make the points of the stars disappear. The appropriate size of the print will depend on the size of strips that are being used.

In most of my projects I make a swatch card of the fabrics I have chosen. Cut a small piece of each fabric. Group them by stars and background. Tape, glue, or staple the swatches to a note card and label them so that you can easily reference what fabric is used for which part of the quilt.

New Quilter?   Because of the constant turnover of fabric lines, you may not be able to find the exact fabrics to make the quilt as shown in a book or magazine. However, a quilt shop assistant can help you to find similar color, value, and design or guide you in making changes to create your own selections. With online shopping becoming so popular, be cautious and keep in mind that what you see on the screen may not be what you expect because of color variation and print sizes.

The Right Tools – Easier Sewing

You will need the basic tools for rotary cutting including:
- ❏ rotary cutter
- ❏ mat
- ❏ 6" x 12" acrylic ruler
- ❏ Clearview Triangle™ 60° ruler 8", 10" or 12"

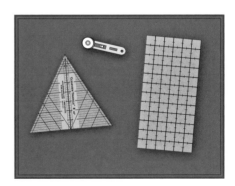

The Clearview Triangle is the one used in all of the illustrations and best fits the instructions. If you use a different one, check your pieces to be sure you have cut the correct shape. Most of the designs can be made using the 8" ruler and are noted as such.

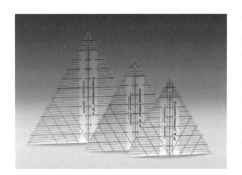

Clearview Triangle™; 8", 10", 12"
Available at www.aliciasattic.com

Those designs that are easier with either the 10" or 12" Clearview Triangle rulers have a note at the beginning of the project. Instructions are given on how to use the 8" ruler with an additional straight ruler to make the longer cuts on page 113. If you have the Clearview Super 60, you can use it for the 60° cuts but will need another straight ruler for other steps.

For sewing you will need your basic supplies including:
- ❏ sewing machine
- ❏ scissors
- ❏ pins
- ❏ thread

I recommend a medium gray or beige shade of thread. However, on designs such as Stars & Stripes and Carolina Lily, you may need to use white and be sure your tension is set correctly so that the white stitches do not show on the dark fabrics.

Rotary Cutting How-to

Here are some guidelines that will help with easy, successful cutting:

- • Double-fold the fabric so that you are making a short cut that is easier to control.

- • Align the fabric, ruler and your body so that your entire arm is in line with the cut. This may mean stepping to the side with each additional cut.

- • Hold your hand like a spider over the ruler, with one or two fingers at the edge of the ruler opposite the edge you are cutting along.

New Quilter?   Working with a rotary cutter makes the process of quilting even easier if you know how to use them with safety and success in mind.

Number one rule: Always close the blade cover after each cut!

Number two rule: Keep the blade sharp. Just as with knives, a sharp blade is safer because it doesn't require too much pressure.

Number three rule: Always cut away from yourself and never toward someone.

To avoid getting a crooked strip, rotary cut as follows:

1. Make the first fold by bringing selvages together so they are parallel and the fabric lays flat.

Selvages

First (single) fold

2. Make the second fold by covering the selvages with the first fold. By covering the selvages, you only see what needs to be seen. Be sure the second fold is smooth.

The key to a straight cut is that both first and second folds are parallel to each other.

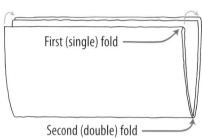

First (single) fold

Second (double) fold

3. Align the ruler along the lower fold and be sure the top fold runs parallel to a ruler line along the section of fabric to be cut into strips. With the ruler at the right end of the fabric and rule lines parallel to the folds, trim the raw edges of all four layers.

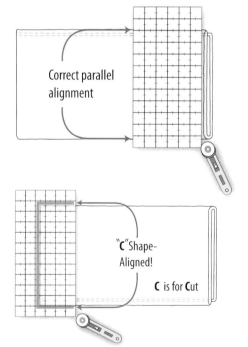

Correct parallel alignment

4. Turn the mat around so that the cut edge is to the left. Be careful not to move the cut edge. To cut strips, align the correct rule line along the cut edge, and have the folds parallel to rule lines. Check this 'C' shape before each cut to guarantee no 'V'. When they don't all align, repeat Step 3.

"C" Shape- Aligned!

C is for **C**ut

The 'V' happens when one fold is not parallel. The diagram shows the extra triangle of fabric which causes the crooked strip. To correct, bring lower end up, and higher end down. You will always know before you cut that the strips will be straight!

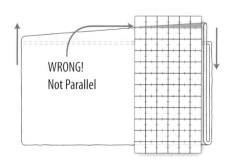

WRONG! Not Parallel

Achieve Perfect Seams

New Quilter? When sewing many seams, it is best to chain the pieces together as illustrated at left. Your sewing machine can handle taking a few stitches that are not in the fabric as long as there is some fabric under the presser foot.

The designs have been written assuming that when the seams have been sewn and pressed only ¼" has been taken away from the front side of each of the fabric pieces. Therefore, on the back they are slightly less than ¼". This is what is meant by sewing with a scant ¼" seam. Most of the designs in this book are quite forgiving if a different seam allowance is taken and even when they are not that consistent. Only the Star of David and City Lights require precision piecing.

Want a Tip? In my own experience of quilting, I did not achieve a "perfect" seam allowance until only recently. I don't have a lot of time to dedicate to perfection in my quilts and therefore have been satisfied with the levels needed for my samples. However, I am always looking for a better way and have found several tools that make my sewing perfect with less effort and time. I use Qtools™ Corner Cut to measure and Qtools Sewing Edge to mark a scant ¼" on my sewing machine. The Sewing Edge provides a stop for the fabric to be guided along as it approaches the foot and needle. It is faster, easier, and more consistent than other marking/guiding methods which I have tried. These two tools together enable me to sew the same seam allowance on any machine.

Qtools Sewing Edge™ and Corner Cut 60°
Available at www.aliciasattic.com

Pressing Pointers

Press seams in the direction the arrows point. This is not always to the darker fabric. The directions are chosen so that seams will lock in place on successive seams and allow for easily matched points with less time required for pinning.

In the strip-sets, those that are cut into left half-blocks have seams that are pressed toward outer strips. Right strip-sets are pressed in toward center strip. Remember this to keep organized throughout the process. Here is a saying which one of my students coined, "Come **right in** or you'll be **left out** in the cold."

To press:

1. Set the seam, pressing as the seam was sewn, with the fabric on top that the seam will be pressed towards. If the seam is toward the dark, have the dark on top.

2. Lift the top fabric slightly, keeping the seam allowance fixed to the ironing surface. Let the top fabric "roll" back over the seam allowance. Don't pull on the fabric such that the seam allowance moves or twists.

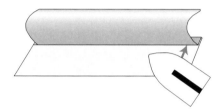

3. Start with the iron flat on the bottom fabric and move the iron across the strip toward the seam, letting the edge of the iron push the top fabric over the seam. Don't muscle the iron which will stretch the fabric.

4. Once across the seam, pick up the iron and move it down to the next section of the bottom fabric and repeat the movement in Step 3.

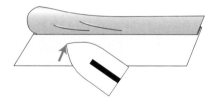

Want a Tip?   When pressing, I recommend having a surface that allows the fabrics to hold in place such as a cotton ticking or cotton flannel. I use a large piece of flannel that is folded into 4 to 8 layers which "covers" my ironing board. I am careful not to have too much padding either. Otherwise, the iron can't push against the edge of the fabric.

In my teaching I have used a wide variety of irons. These features are best for the technique that I use:

No auto-off ✦ Not too heavy ✦ Good steam without leaking ✦ Edge of sole plate not too square, not too round. ✦ Shape of iron has a long, "straight" section.

With these features and the cotton ironing surface, I can iron easily, with steam, and not have any stretching of the fabric. Even better, the iron is doing the work and I don't get my fingers too close to the heat.

Index of Designs

Index of Designs

All Stars

61" x 80"

Pieced & Quilted by Marci Baker

Fabrics Selected and Provided by Tennessee Quilts

Key to symbols:
FW: Full Width of fabric
1/2W: Half Width
1/4W: Quarter Width

Recommended Tools:
8" Clearview Triangle (Minimum)

These quilts bring a smile to my face every time I see them not only because they are one of my favorite designs, but they also include groupings of colors that make me feel good! Whether you choose fabrics off the bolt or use a variety of scraps, you can easily make a blanket of stars to sleep under with these user-friendly instructions. This quilt is made from a wide variety of fabrics; in fact, more than 40. I recommend using a similar number if possible to achieve the richness of the design like Nanette did in her fall rendition shown on the back cover. However, I realize not everyone has the fabric available or is comfortable making that many decisions. Gather your favorite fabrics and select values close to each other for stars. Then for background, select one or more fabrics that are similar to each other but significantly different in value from the stars. At a minimum choose at least 12 star fabrics. Now you are ready to make a favorite quilt of your own.

Note that the size of strip needed from any one fabric is either one 2 ½" x FW strip or one 3" x FW strip (or equivalent 1/2W strips). This makes the design great for the popular pre-cut strips or cutting some from each of your fat quarters. See the cutting instructions for the total number of strips required, page 20.

Fabric Yardage

S* Stars	Bk** Background	Border1	Border 2	Binding	Backing
(12) ⅜ yd ea.	(3) ¾ yd ea.	½ yd	1½ yd	⅝ yd	3 ¾ yd

* For a look similar to the photograph I recommend choosing (36) ⅛ yd star fabrics and (5) ½ yd background fabrics.
**For using only one fabric for background you need 2½ yd.

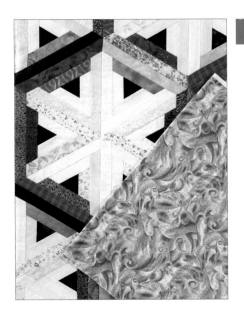

New Quilter? If you are not sure when choosing a large number of fabrics, select a multi-color print that you like as your palette print. Now use it to find the "scraps" for your quilt. This way you have a grouping of many colors and you know that you like them together. The quilt will have a scrappy feel but with a plan.

Know what values you need for your design, and pick the fabrics based on the value needed for the design and from the colors in your palette print. Choosing three or more of each different color will help the fabrics blend.

Surprisingly, I do not include the palette print in the final pieced top. However, I have put this fabric as part of the back of the quilt to show how the fabrics were selected. Here is an example from *Not Your Grandmother's Log Cabin*™ where I used this method.

Designing Quilter? You can make this quilt larger with the following information. Each row of stars added on the length adds 6". Each star added on the width adds 7". Each FW star set of 18 strips makes 24 stars. For even more details on changing quilt sizes, check out the Designer Section, page 103.

Cut Strips

From the variety of star fabrics and background fabrics cut the strips as follows:

Size	S	Bk
3" x FW	12 total	6 total
2½" x FW	24 total	12 total

Cut all of these strips into 1/2W, so that you have even numbers of each 3" fabric strip and are working with similar lengths of strips.

Sew Strip-Sets

Group the strips together into (6) 1/2W star sets, each of which will consist of 6 strip-sets using the following information.

If you are using only 12 star fabrics, the design will look better by planning where the fabrics appear. Note in the diagram where the fabrics need to be placed in the star set in order to fall in the desired position in the star. Group the strip-sets and label them as Star Set 1: $A_L A_R$, B_L…, and Star Set 2: A_L… etc., to keep organized.

2 ½" Star Sets: 1/2W of 6 combinations or equivalent in 1/4W

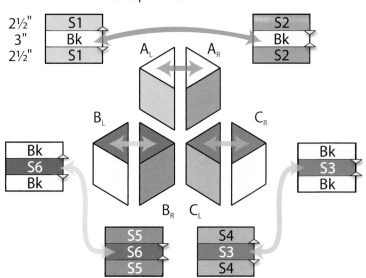

If you are using 18 or more star fabrics, you can randomly pick your fabrics for the sets and not be concerned with where a specific star fabric falls. If you want to mix the fabrics even more, cut all of the strips again into 1/4W and make more variety of combinations, which is how the quilt shown was made.

A few rules to note:

1. The center strips (3") for each block, A, B, or C have to match. In other words, center strip for A_L needs to be the exact same fabric as center strip for A_R. This is true for B_L and B_R, and C_L and C_R, too.

2. The outer strips of a set do not have to match each other (but can if desired). I recommend grouping the strips before sewing so that the fabrics are distributed evenly throughout the

design. Now that you have them grouped, sew the strip-sets together remembering that the 3" strips are in the middle and 2 ½" strips on both sides. Strip-sets should measure 7" across but the method is flexible. Be as consistent as possible and the pieces will work.

Cut Shapes

Cut 2 ½" half-blocks of quantity shown in diagram using instructions for left on page 108 and for right on page 109.

2½" Left

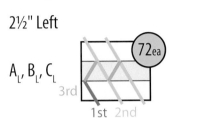

A$_L$, B$_L$, C$_L$

2½" Right

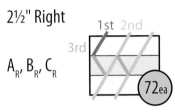

A$_R$, B$_R$, C$_R$

EITHER Single Background Fabric
For filling in edges from the background fabric cut the following using instructions on page 112 and 114.

2 ½" Half-Hexagons
(using 4¾" rule line)

Bk: 2 Strips
7" x FW

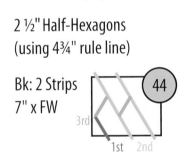

2¾" Half-Triangles (half L, half R)

Bk: 1 Strip
2½" x FW

OR Multiple Background Fabrics
Cut the following strips from the variety of background fabrics:

Size	Bk
3" x 1/2W	4
2 ½" x 1/2W	8

Cut these strips in half again into 1/4W strips. With 3" in the middle and 2 ½" on each side, sew into (8) 1/4W strip-sets with center strips matching in pairs. Press one of each 3" center strip as left, and the matching center strip as right.

2 ½" Sets: 1/4 W, 4 Left, 4 Right

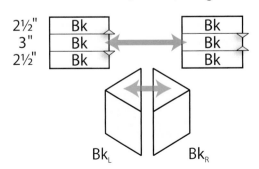

Multiple Background Fabrics (continued)
Cut 2 ½" half-blocks of quantity shown in diagram using instructions for left on page 108 and for right on page 109. Also cut the edge pieces from the variety of background fabric as shown on page 114.

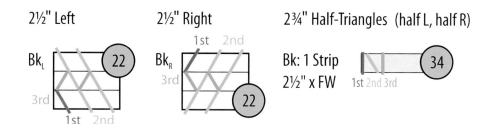

Layout

Lay out the pieces following the diagram, noting the sample is 3 stars by 5 stars and the actual quilt is 7 stars by 11 stars. Notice how the stars are "sideways" on the finished quilt. This final orientation makes the stars stand out even more. Watch for too many of one fabric in a location to keep the colors evenly spaced. Piece together in columns and press seams according to diagram, referring to pages 115 - 117 if more detail is needed. Sew columns together in pairs (pressing consistently in one direction), then pairs together until the top is completed. Square the top by trimming just past the star points, leaving a ¼" seam allowance.

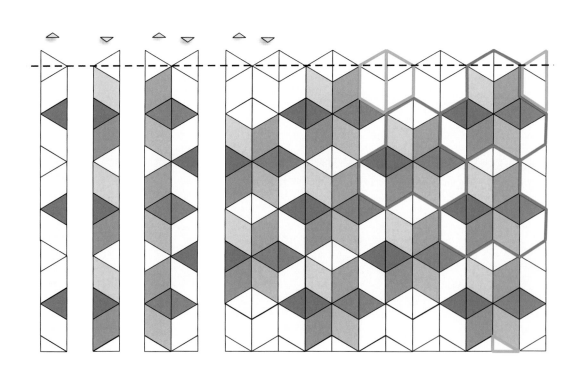

Borders, Backing, Quilting, and Binding

Use the following measurements to add borders and to prepare backing and binding. For detailed instructions on each of these steps, see pages 118 - 126.

Size	Border 1	Border 2	Binding	Backing
1½" x FW	7	-	-	(2) 1⅞ yd
5½" x FW	-	8	-	
Your favorite size, pg 123	-	-	7-8	

Quilt as shown in diagram with lines that are a single curve across each star point and a small double curve between stars. Be consistent with direction of the curves and make a grid of 3 different directions as indicated by the colored lines. You can also consider designs throughout the book.

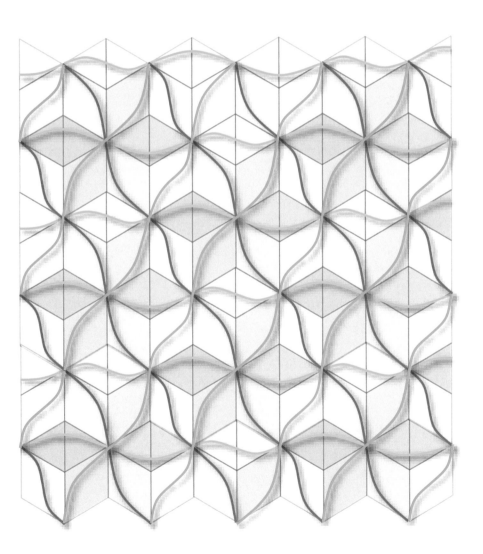

Brenda's Stars *60" x 71"*

Pieced by Brenda Backx ✶ Quilted by Marci Baker

Ｎo, this is not your Grandmother's quilt! Believe it or not, star blocks streak across the quilt in a rainbow of reproduction fabrics. Capturing a piece of the past has become very popular since the late 1980s when reproduction fabrics were milled just for quilters. Visit your local quilt shop or browse online for a wide selection of these fabrics. These Rising Star blocks will look beautiful in any color palette. The instructions for this quilt are written for a slightly scrappy look, just as if Grandma stitched it from clothing scraps.

Fabric Yardage

S1 Star 1	S2 Star 2	Bk Background	Border	Binding	Backing
(7) ¼ yd ea.	(7) ¼ yd ea.	2 yd	2 yd	¾ yd	3¾ yd

Cut Strips

Cut the strips as follows:

Size	S1	S2	Bk
2½" x FW	1 of ea.	1 of ea.	7
2" x FW	2 of ea.	2 of ea.	14

2" Star Sets: 1/2W of 7 combinations

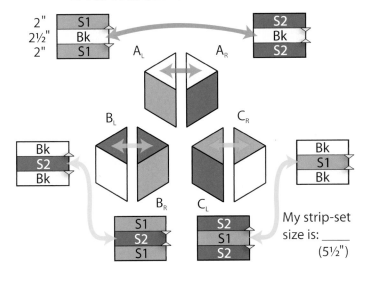

My strip-set size is: _____
(5½")

Sew Strip-Sets

Cut all of the strips into 1/2W. Group 7 star sets as shown in the diagram, pairing an S1 with an S2 for each. Sew the strip-sets as shown in the diagram. Strip-sets should measure 5½" across. Measure your strip-set size and make note of it. Be as consistent as possible and the pieces will work.

Cut Shapes

Cut 2" half-blocks of quantity shown in diagram using instructions for left on page 108 and for right on page 109.

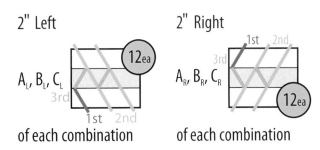

2" Left

A_L, B_L, C_L

12ea

1st 2nd 3rd

of each combination

2" Right

A_R, B_R, C_R

1st 2nd 3rd

12ea

of each combination

Cut the following shapes from the strips indicated in the diagram or from your strip-set size. If more information is needed see page 112.

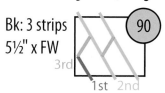

2" Half-Hexagons   (using 3¾" rule line)

Bk: 3 strips
5½" x FW

90

3rd

1st   2nd

or My strip-set size_____

Layout

Lay out the left and right half-blocks into the stars using the diagram, noticing how the stars are "sideways" on the finished quilt. The sample is 3 stars x 4 stars, whereas the quilt is 9 stars x 8 stars. You can lay the stars out in the diagonal form or mix it up. Place background pieces in-between stars as shown. To fill in along one edge, use half-hexagons which have been cut approximately in half. Sew the pieces into long strips and sew strips together in pairs, pages 115 - 117. Join to complete the top. Square the top by trimming just past the star points, leaving a ¼" seam allowance.

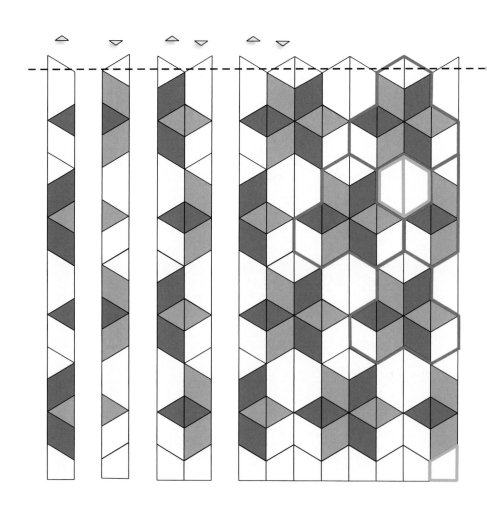

Borders, Backing, Quilting, and Binding

Use the following measurements to add borders and to prepare backing and binding. For detailed instructions on each of these steps, see pages 118 - 126.

Size	Border	Binding	Backing
10" x FW	6	-	(2) 1⅞ yd
Your favorite size, pg 123	-	6-7	

Quilt as shown in the illustration with lines outlining the stars and/or petals in the stars. Follow the different colors red, yellow, green, to see the continuous lines that are used; or consider other options pictured throughout the book.

For the border design, I made several grids to see how to go around the corner. When quilting, I decided not to "mark" the lines, but put a grid on the border edges with painter's masking tape. I made a tick mark at each inch on the tape and adjusted some to make an even number. Then I used my drawing as a guide while quilting on my Pfaff sewing machine. The border would not win ribbons at a show, but the quilt was made for snuggling under so that is ok by me. The border design was a learning opportunity to try a new design and method. Next time I will mark with dots on the border fabric, but not the entire line. I have an easier time moving the quilt point to point, and I will not have to remove a lot of marks. This gives me more time for the next project.

Carolina Lily   *40" x 40"*

Pieced & Quilted by Bobbie Crosby

This pattern first appeared in the United States in the early 1840s. Since that time, quilters have chosen numerous layout and color variations. The number of petals and blossoms can vary depending upon the whim of the quilter. The actual Carolina Lily flower grows across the southeastern states and has been designated as the official state wildflower of North Carolina. It has yellow to reddish-orange petals with dark spots. Following historical tradition, however, red and green are the usual colors quilters select when making a Carolina Lily quilt.

Inspired by the quilts in *Treasury of American Quilts* by Cyril I. Nelson and Carter Houck, I added my own touch to this block, which resulted in this quilt made by Bobbie Crosby. I designed these flowers to consist of 4-petal blossoms with appliquéd stems and leaves with a coordinating blossom and leaf border. Using solid red and green on a muslin background gives the feeling of the 1920s-30s designs.

Designing Quilter? Try this simple table runner which was made by Bobbie in some of her favorite colors. Visit www.aliciasattic.com/book-addenda/index.html for detailed instructions.

Table Runner - 16"x 46"
Pieced & quilted by Bobbie Crosby

Fabric Yardage

F Flower	L Leaf	Bk Background	Binding	Backing
⅝ yd	⅝ yd	1½ yd	½ yd	1¼ yd*

*If your fabric width is narrower than 42" you need 2 ½ yds.

Cut Strips

Cut the strips as follows:

Size	F	L	Bk
5" x FW	-	-	1
3" x FW	3	-	1
2½" x FW	2	3	6

CAROLINA LILY

2-1/2" Star Sets: FW

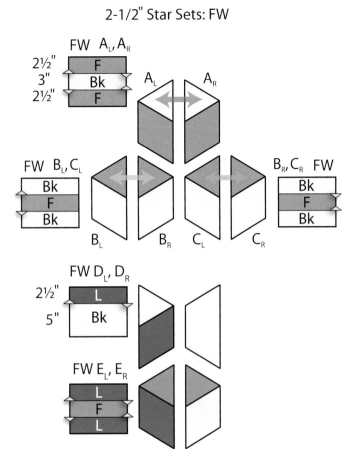

FW A_L, A_R

2½"
3"
2½"

FW B_L, C_L

FW B_R, C_R

FW D_L, D_R

2½"
5"

FW E_L, E_R

Sew Strip-Sets

Because of the arrangement of the flower and background fabrics through the flowers and borders, there are some pieces that are needed less than others. The strip-sets will be shorter for those.

With 3″ strips in the middle and 2 ½″ strips on both sides, sew the strip-sets as shown in the diagram. To save time, the 5″ background strip replaces a combination of 3″ and 2 ½″ strips. For this design, both left and right halves are cut from the same set for A block and borders. Find the center point of the A block and border strip-sets and snip the seam allowance. Press one end with seams in, the other end with seams out. For blocks B & C, the strip-sets are pressed as noted. Strip-sets should measure 7″ across.

Cut Shapes

Fold the A strip-set in half, wrong sides together, locking/matching the seams. Cut 2 ½″ half blocks of the quantity shown in the diagram. Place B & C strip-sets wrong sides together. Follow directions for the side that is right side up (on top), either left with the seams pressed out, page 108, or right with the seams pressed in, page 109. For the set with the 5″ strip, be sure that when the slice is cut in half, both pieces are the same size.

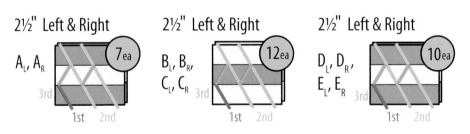

2½" Left & Right

A_L, A_R   7 ea
3rd   1st   2nd

2½" Left & Right

B_L, B_R,   12 ea
C_L, C_R   3rd
1st   2nd

2½" Left & Right

D_L, D_R,   10 ea
E_L, E_R   3rd
1st   2nd

Cut the following shapes from the strips indicated in the diagram. If more information is needed see pages 111 and 112.

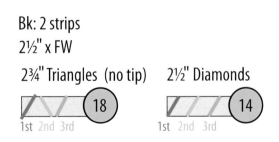

Bk: 2 strips
2½" x FW

2¾" Triangles (no tip)   2½" Diamonds

1st 2nd 3rd   18   1st 2nd 3rd   14

Sew Blocks

Lay out the left and right half-blocks into Carolina Lily stars using the diagram. Fill in edges with triangle and diamond shapes. Sew the pieces into strips, sew strips together in pairs, and pairs into the block, see pages 115 - 117.

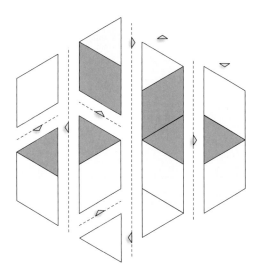

Appliqué the leaves and stem to each block by hand or machine. Use 1½" wide bias strips for stems and your favorite appliqué method. See references on page 127 for further information.

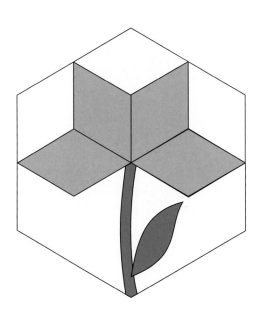

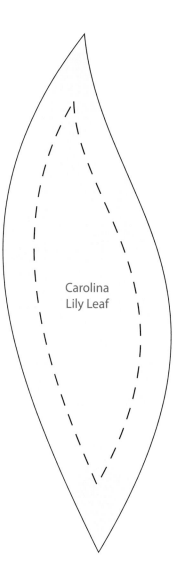

Carolina
Lily Leaf

Cut Setting Pieces

Prior to cutting these next pieces, measure your blocks and make adjustments if needed.

Bk: 2 strips, 4½" x FW

4¾" Triangles (no tip)   4¾" Half-Triangles   (half L, half R)

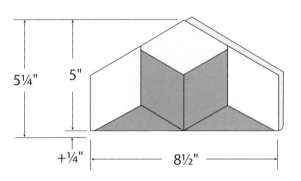

1st 2nd 3rd   16   1st 2nd 3rd   4

Fold a block in half matching bottom point to top point. Measure from the point to the fold and add ¼". This should be 5 ¼". Measure the block side to side. This should be 8 ½". Cut 1 rectangle of background fabric, either 5 ¼" x 8 ½" or use your adjusted numbers.

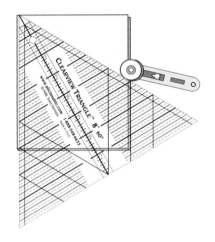

5¼"   5"   8½"
+¼"

Fold rectangle in half side to side (widthwise). Align edge of ruler along fold and point of ruler at top of fold. Cut along top edge of ruler. Check that this fits your blocks, then cut 3 more pieces.

Layout

Lay out the blocks and setting pieces as illustrated. Sew setting pieces onto edges of blocks, sew into rows, and sew rows together.

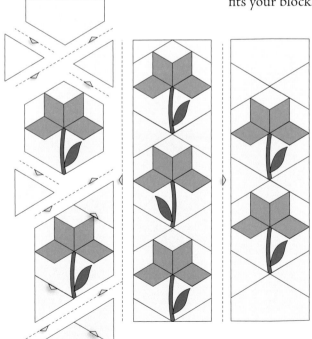

Borders

Use the remaining pieces to make 2 left side borders and 2 right side borders. These are mirror image of each other. See diagram for placement.

Fit the pieced borders to the center section by measuring and cutting filler borders. Either mark or trim ends of pieced borders at 45° angles, measured from outer edge and outer corner. See border at right side of diagram.

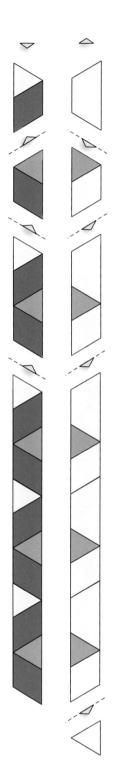

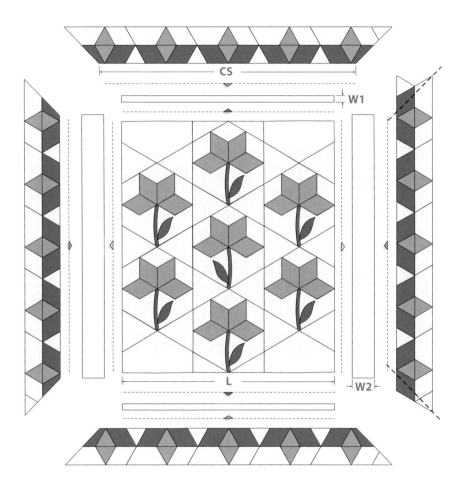

Measure and find average length of pieced borders along inside edge. This is the size the center section needs to be in both directions. My Center Size (**CS**) is: _____.

Measure the pieced center, top to bottom in a couple of places. Use the average. Subtract average center length from **CS**. Divide this amount by 2 and add ½″ for seam allowance. This is the width to cut for the top and bottom strips. (**W1** = _____).

For the length (**L**) of these strips, measure the pieced center, side to side in a couple of places. Use the average. (**L** = _____). Cut two filler borders to the size of **W1** x **L**.

Sew background filler borders to top and bottom. Press seams away from center.

Using the side-to-side measurement, **L**, from above, subtract **L** from **CS**. Divide the amount by 2 and add ½" for seam allowance. This is the width to cut for the side strips. (**W2** = _____). The length is **CS**.

Cut two filler borders to the size of **W2** x **CS**. Sew background filler borders to sides. Press seams away from center. Add pieced borders to center section, mitering at corners. See page 119 for more detail about miters. Press seams in toward center.

Backing, Quilting, and Binding

Use the following measurements to prepare backing and binding. For detailed instructions on each of these steps, see pages 120 - 126.

Size	Binding	Backing
Your favorite size, pg 123	5	(1) 1¼ yd

For quilting, Bobbie stitched in the ditch around each flower and stippled the background. Consider the illustration below, or other options pictured throughout the book, for choosing your quilt design. Follow red, yellow, then green for continuous stitching.

Oh My Stars!

Christmas Wreath

26" x 30"

Pieced & Quilted by Marci Baker

Key to symbols:
FW: Full Width of fabric
1/2W: Half Width
1/4W: Quarter Width

Recommended Tools:
10" Clearview Triangle (Minimum)

Visitors will be awed by this Christmas wreath when they come knocking on your door. The friendly instructions will guide you in creating a colorful holiday decoration, which can also be used to deck your halls, of course. I have "woven" a virtual ribbon through the star blocks, and then attached a bow with the same red fabric. Depending upon your color choices, the stars may be subtle or obvious.

A light color version (below, left) is also pictured to help you decide which color way you may want to try. The background fabric in this wreath was designed by Gail de Marcken based on her illustrations in the children's book *The Quiltmaker's Gift* by Jeff Brumbeau. This poignant story reflects upon the joy of giving gifts versus the yearning of wanting everything. So pick up some Christmas fabric and design your own to keep or give away. Or, try other fabrics for a year-round display.

Fabric Yardage			
S Star	R Ribbon	Bk Background	Backing
½ yd	1 yd	¾ yd	1 yd

Cut Strips

Cut the strips as follows:

Size	S	R	Bk
3½" x FW	1	1	1
3" x FW	2	1	5

From these strips cut the following:

Size	S	R	Bk
3½" x 1/2W	1	-	1
3½" x 1/4W	2	2	1
3" x 1/2W	2	-	2
3" x 1/4W	4	4	2

Sew Strip-Sets

Because of the arrangement of the ribbon fabric through the stars and the other parts of the star being the same, there are some pieces that are needed less than others. The strip-sets will be shorter for those. There are 5 combinations that use the 1/4W strips. Note that this particular strip length is a tight fit to the pieces needed. Align the ends as straight as possible when you are sewing. Selvages may need to be used in the seam allowance depending on the actual width of your fabric.

Christmas Wreath 24" x 28"
Pieced & Quilted by Alicia Sanchez

With 3½" strips in the middle and 3" strips on both sides, sew the strip-sets as shown in the diagram. For this design, both left and right halves are cut from the same set. Find the center point of the sets and snip the seam allowance. Press one end with seams in, the other end with seams out. Sets should measure 8½" across. Be as consistent as possible and the pieces will work.

Cut Shapes

Left and right half-blocks, 3" size, are cut simultaneously from each strip-set. Fold the strip-set in half, wrong sides together, locking/matching the seams. Follow directions for the side that is right side up (on top), either left with the seams pressed out, page 108, or right with the seams pressed in, page 109.

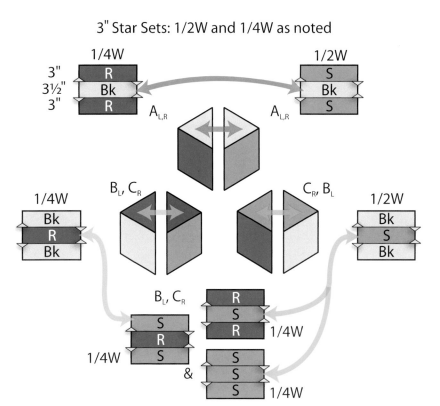

3" Star Sets: 1/2W and 1/4W as noted

Because this is a tight fit, start the cutting at the fold end and trim off the least possible. Cut the number shown in the diagram based on the length of the strip-set.

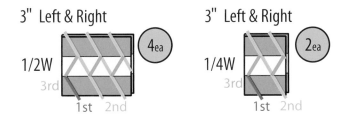

3" Left & Right 1/2W 4ea
3rd 1st 2nd

3" Left & Right 1/4W 2ea
3rd 1st 2nd

Cut the following shapes from the remaining 3" background strips. If more information is needed see pages 111-112.

Bk: 2 strips, 3" x FW

3¼" Triangles (no tip) 8
1st 2nd 3rd

3" Diamonds 8
1st 2nd 3rd

5¾" Trapezoids/Flat Pyramids 4
1st 2nd 3rd

Layout

Lay out the left and right half-blocks into the wreath shape using the two diagrams. Fill in edges with cut background shapes outlined in red. Sew the pieces into long strips and press seams, alternating direction with each row. Sew strips together in pairs, pages 115 - 117. Join to complete the top.

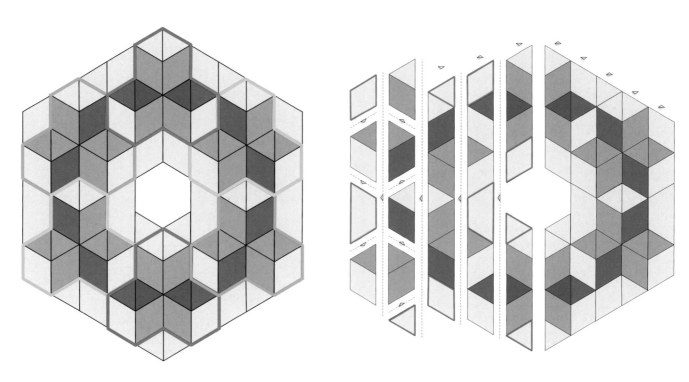

Quilting

Layer and quilt the wreath for dimensionality using a layer or two of wool or fluffy polyester batting, and for stiffness have a layer of Quilter's Dream Cotton Supreme, below this. I recommend basting around the edge when working with this thickness and for applying binding later. Consider the quilt design shown or try your own design, as did Alicia in her off-white version. Here is her original angel design. Follow the red, yellow, then green for continuous quilting.

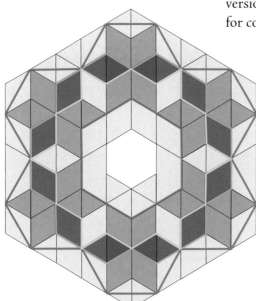

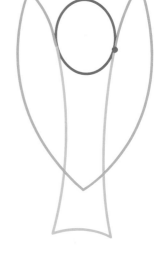

Binding

Finish the edges with binding as follows:

Use strips for binding that are 1¾" to 2½" wide depending on batting thickness. Fold in half and apply like traditional binding, mitering outside corners following binding instructions on page 123. Grade away some of the bulk of the batting layers, if needed.

For inside corners, clip to basting and straighten the seams while applying the binding. On the inside there is not enough room to sew a traditional join at the ends, so fold ends in and hand stitch folds together, when hand stitching the binding to the back.

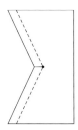

Straighten while stitching

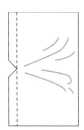

Bow

For the bow, cut (2) 7"x 30" strips of ribbon fabric. Join at the ends to make one strip. Fold in half right sides together. At the ends, trim 60° angles. Stitch raw edges together leaving an opening near the middle for turning. Trim corners. Turn right side out, press, and stitch closed. Accordian fold and stitch the center of the bow to the wreath with back stitching to reinforce it. Tie the bow.

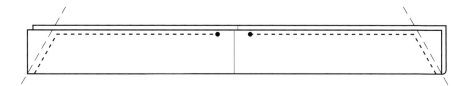

For hanging, attach a plastic ring at center back. If needed for support, attach piano wire or similar thin flexible rod on back between upper corners.

When storing the wreath, remove the support rod and untie the bow, fold ends in and roll the wreath onto an empty wrapping-paper tube with right sides out and tissue paper or scrap fabric on the outside. Do not forget to include the rod in the packaging. Hope you enjoyed creating this one-of-a-kind holiday decoration, and may you find joy and peace during your holidays and throughout the year!

City Lights *42" x 58"*

Pieced by Scott Hansen ✷ Quilted by Marci Baker

Key to symbols:
FW: Full Width of fabric (~40")
1/2W: Half Width (~20")
1/4W: Quarter Width (~10")
1/8W: Eighth Width (~5")

Recommended Tools:
10" Clearview Triangle (Minimum)

Want something a little more contemporary? Scott rose to the occasion with this challenge. With little more than a sketch I provided and a flurry of long-distance discussions, he pulled together this amazing nightscape featuring star blocks drifting over the city. His artistic eye is wonderfully evident by the array of fabrics he used. The stars seem to sparkle from the highest cloud level to the peaks of the skyscrapers. The darker tones of the various prints clearly define each structure and, in contrast, the lighter fabric designs brighten the building facades as if all the lights were turned on after the sun went down.

When selecting your fabrics, keep in mind that the star fabrics should be close to each other in value and significantly different than the background. Avoid directional fabrics for the sky. The sky value shades gradually with the lighter shades being a good contrast to the tops of the building. Scott also used contrast in hue to help the structures stand out. Choose variations with light, medium, and dark contrast for each building. Work with some solid fabrics and some larger print fabrics. Look for stripes and geometric prints rather than florals. Many of the modern designer fabrics lend themselves to this effect.

Because this design is meant to be individualized, there will be many options for you to change to make this your own. In fact, Scott used his own shapes for filling in between the stars to change the transitions of fabrics. I have given instructions for a more repetitive process for cutting and sewing. There are seams where you are sewing the same fabrics back together. However, I have found that with more evenly spaced seams, the quilt will piece together more easily and more likely lay flat. Also, the equal size fabric pieces give a similar texture throughout.

Fabric Yardage

S* Star	Bdg** Buildings	Bk Background	G Ground	Binding	Backing
(13) of ⅛ yd ea	(15) L (14) M (14) D ⅛ yd ea.	(5) ¾ yd ea.	½ yd	½ yd	2¾ yd

* Need at least 1½ yd. total if using fewer star fabrics.

** Various sizes, ranging from 4½" x 5½" to 4½" x 24". See page 46 for exact sizes. Need at least 1 yd. of Light (L), ¾ yd. Medium (M), and ½ yd. Dark (D) for buildings.

Cut Strips

From the stars and background fabrics cut strips as follows: Note that there will be some 4" strips cut later.

Size	S	Bk1	Bk2	Bk3	Bk4	Bk5
2" x FW	1 ea.*	1	1	1	1	1
1½" x FW	1 ea.*	1	2	2	1	1

* Minimum of (5) 2" x FW and (9) 1½" x FW if fewer star fabrics.

Cut these strips into 1/8W as needed to make the following strip-sets.

1½" Star Sets (1 star fabric): 1/8W, 7 total
with Bk1:1, Bk2:2, Bk3:2, Bk4:1, Bk5:1

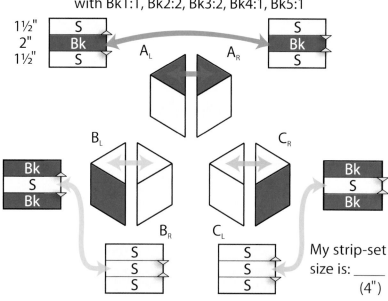

Sew Strip-Sets

Group the strips together into ten 1/8W star sets with either 1 star fabric or 2 star fabrics as listed in the diagram. Sew the sets together. After pressing as shown in the diagram, measure several to get your average strip-set size.

My strip-set size is: _____
(4")

1½" Star Sets (2 fabrics): 1/8W, 3 total
with Bk2:1, Bk3:2

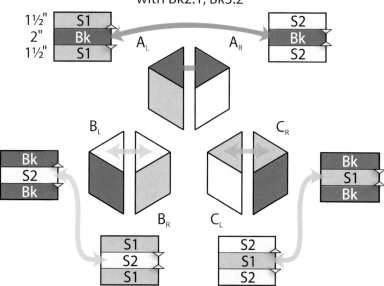

CITY LIGHTS

Cut Shapes

Cut 1½" half-blocks of quantity shown in diagram for each of the 10 star sets, using instructions for left on page 108 and for right on page 109.

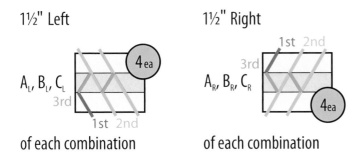

1½" Left

A_L, B_L, C_L

4 ea

of each combination

1½" Right

A_R, B_R, C_R

4 ea

of each combination

Cut the following shapes from the strips indicated in the diagrams. (Triangles are cut without tips). Use your own strip-set size in place of the 4" if yours is different. If more information on cutting is needed see page 111 - 113.

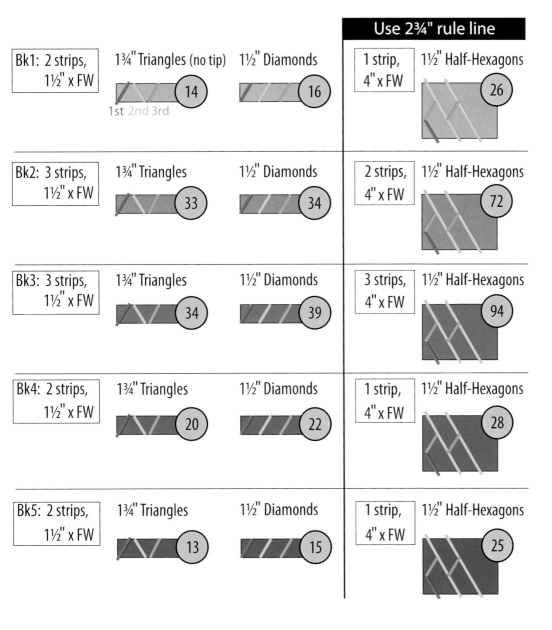

Use 2¾" rule line

Bk1: 2 strips, 1½" x FW	1¾" Triangles (no tip) 14	1½" Diamonds 16	1 strip, 4" x FW	1½" Half-Hexagons 26
Bk2: 3 strips, 1½" x FW	1¾" Triangles 33	1½" Diamonds 34	2 strips, 4" x FW	1½" Half-Hexagons 72
Bk3: 3 strips, 1½" x FW	1¾" Triangles 34	1½" Diamonds 39	3 strips, 4" x FW	1½" Half-Hexagons 94
Bk4: 2 strips, 1½" x FW	1¾" Triangles 20	1½" Diamonds 22	1 strip, 4" x FW	1½" Half-Hexagons 28
Bk5: 2 strips, 1½" x FW	1¾" Triangles 13	1½" Diamonds 15	1 strip, 4" x FW	1½" Half-Hexagons 25

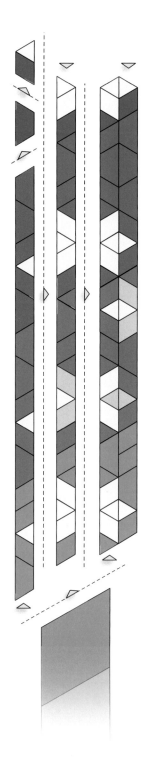

Stars Layout

Lay out the pieces following the diagram on page 45 which shows only the stars section with the first pieces of each building.

Want a Tip? The direction of the grain is not critical when laying out these triangles and diamonds. However, I prefer to position straight grain along a diagonal edge rather than the vertical edges. This allows the pieces to ease as needed when matching the points.

For each column, sew the pieces together according to the order shown in the expanded layout. When seams will be pressed down, begin piecing at top and end at the bottom. When seams will be pressed up, begin piecing at the bottom and end at the top. This prevents most issues with bulky seam intersections.

Sew the columns into groups of 4 as indicated by the diagram. Press seams consistently one direction. These units will be joined with the building pieces for each of the columns in the next section.

City Lights -
Stars Layout

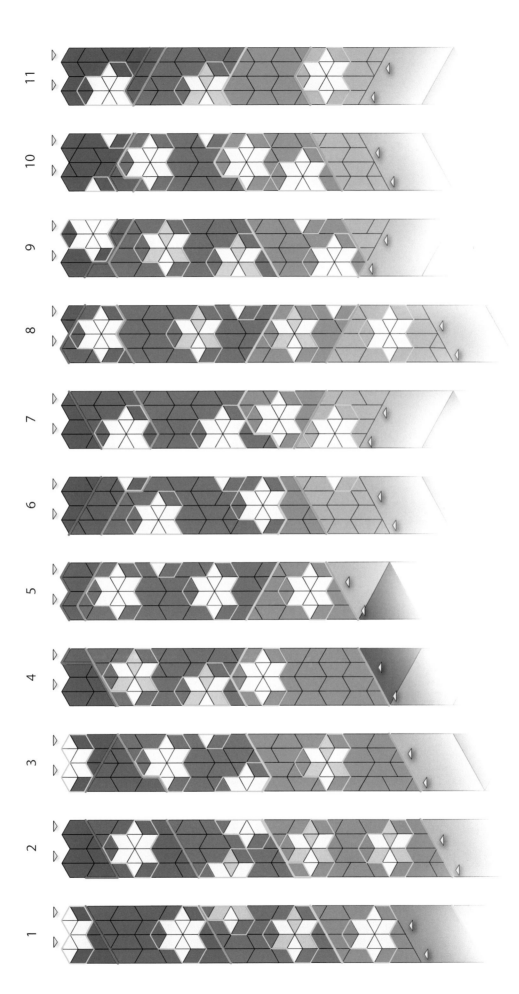

Buildings

Cut Shapes

Measure several of your star units to get a width of your piecing. The building pieces need to match at least within ⅛" in order for the quilt to lay flat. The units should measure 4 ½". However, if yours are ⅛" or more different, follow the tip on the next page.

Select the fabrics to be used for each building. Cut the appropriate shapes for each of the buildings, the sky, and the ground, using the diagram for size and shape. Each should be cut from 4 ½" strips unless you are adjusting to fit your units.

An outline version of this is on our website:
www.aliciasattic.com/book-addenda/index.html

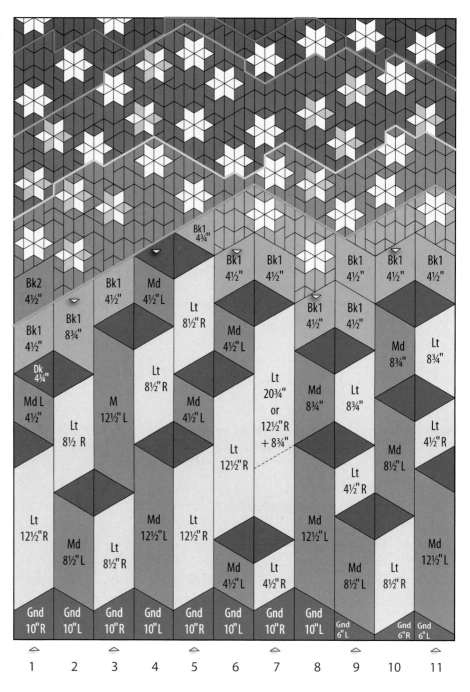

Want a Tip? If your unit size is different than 4½" use the table below to cut your shapes for the buildings that will fit your size. If you are making these adjustments, you are spending extra time and effort to make your project fit. For future projects, I recommend that you try Qtools™ Sewing Edge and Qtools™ Corner Cut to help mark your seam allowance on your machine. I have been amazed at how straight and consistent my seams are now that I use them. I've even learned a faster way to sew strips together. Visit my website, www.aliciasattic.com/book-addenda/index.html, to see a demonstration and make your sewing frustration-free.

Qtools Corner Cut 60°™ and Sewing Edge™

Building Layout

Now that you have the pieces cut, lay out the building shapes and sew into columns. Sew and press in similar direction beginning at the bottom when seams are pressed up. Begin at the top when seams are pressed down. Join these units to the appropriate star units. Sew these last units together to complete the top. Square the top by trimming just past the star points, leaving a ¼" seam allowance.

	Unit Size	Strip Size for Buildings	Shape Size Substitution								
Size in diagram	4½"	4½"	4½"	4¾"	6"	8½"	8¾"	10"	12½"	20¾"
Your Adjusted Size	4⅜"	4⅜"	4⅜"	4⅝"	5⅞"	8¼"	8½"	9¾"	12⅛"	20⅛"
Your Adjusted Size	4¼"	4¼"	4¼"	4½"	5¾"	8"	8¼"	9½"	11¾"	19½"

Backing, Quilting, and Binding

There are no borders on this quilt, but they can definitely be added. Instead, I completed it with a 1/2" wide binding. Use the following measurements to prepare the backing and binding. For detailed instructions on wide binding, see pages 120 - 126.

Size	Binding	Backing
2¾" x FW	5	(2) 1⅜ yd pieces

Quilt as shown in the photo which is an outline of each star and vertical lines up and down on the buildings with crossing lines on the tops. For the buildings I used a variegated thread that was alternating 1" black and white sections which added the look of more lights in the buildings. For the sky I quilted the design shown in Galaxy of Stars, page 60, changing the thread color from dark blue to medium blue to yellow as I worked down the quilt. For the ground I did a cobblestone effect by creating circles attached to each other. This requires quilting over parts of the circle a couple of times, but makes for a very interesting texture. You can choose to make your stones circles or ovals or a variety. Enjoy viewing your City Lights!

First Stars

14" x 26"

Pieced & Quilted by Marci Baker

14" x 28"

Pieced & Hand Quilted by Anita Hartinger

Appropriately named, the quilt on the right was made by a first-time quilter. Anita stitched a striking blue-violet combination that could be used as a wall hanging or table runner. She proudly scored another "first" in her belt by hand-quilting this piece. While the stars are a traditional pattern, the border gives it a contemporary flair that would look great at home or work. Overall, this is a wonderful skill-building design for any first-time quilter.

The quilt on the left is a great example of how color choices affect the finished product. I also decided to take on a different perspective by machine-quilting my project. I accentuated each section of the border and then outlined around the stars using a satin stitch. Wherever you plan to put this quilt, you can make a bold or subtle piece to your room's best advantage depending upon the color and quilting selections you make.

Choose values close together with S2 slightly darker than S1. For the background pick a value significantly different than the star fabrics. This contrast will make the stars pop!

Fabric Yardage				
S1 Star	S2 Star	Bk Background	Binding	Backing
⅜ yd	⅜ yd	⅜ yd	¼ yd	⅝ yd

New Quilter? As noted in the picture, the finished quilts are a different size even though the same instructions were used. You may not always complete a project that ends up the same size as indicated on a pattern. The variance between sewing machines, the quilter's experience in sewing construction, and the thread tension may affect the final product.

Cut Strips

Cut the strips as follows:

Size	S1	S2	Bk
3" x FW	1	1	1
2½" x FW	1	1	1

Cut all of these strips into 1/4W.

2-1/2" Star Sets: 1/4W

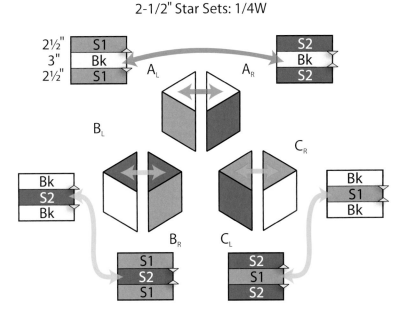

Sew Strip-Sets

Sew with the right sides together using a scant ¼" seam. With 3" strips in the middle and 2 ½" strips on both sides, sew the strip-sets as shown in the diagram. Label according to left or right halves of block A, B, or C. Press in the direction of the arrows. Sets should measure 7" across. Be as consistent as possible and the pieces will work.

New Quilter? You do not need to pin the strips together before sewing. Also, direction of pressing may not seem to be important, but this will make a big difference in how well the points come together and how little, if any, pinning will be needed later.

Cut Shapes

Cut 2 ½" half-blocks of quantity shown in diagram using instructions for left on page 108 and for right on page 109.

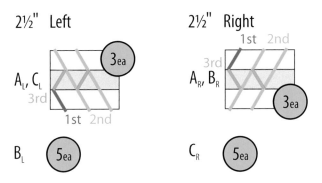

Cut the following shapes from the strips indicated in the diagram. If more information is needed see pages 111 - 112.

Bk: 1 strip
2½" x FW

2¾" Triangles (no tip)   2½" Diamonds

Layout

Lay out 1 star with A half-blocks at the top, B half-blocks at the left, and C half-blocks at the right (red outline). Lay out 2 more stars below the first. **Do not sew star pieces into star shapes.** Fill in sides with extras from B_L and C_R. Use triangles and diamonds to fill in top and bottom edges (green outline).

Sew half-blocks into 4 long strips with scant ¼", pages 115 - 117. Press the seams just sewn in alternate directions with each strip (the seams pressed in the half-blocks are not changed). Sew long strips together in pairs.

Press seams away from center of design. Sew pairs together, pressing seams either way.

Trim ¼" beyond star points for seam allowance.

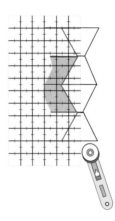

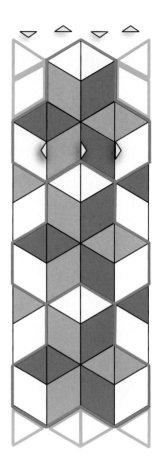

Borders, Backing, Quilting, and Binding

Use the following measurements to add borders and to prepare backing and binding. For detailed instructions on each of these steps, see pages 118 - 126.

Size	S1	S2	Binding	Backing
2½" x FW	1	1	-	(1) ⅝ yd
1½" x FW	1	1	-	
Your favorite size, pg 123	-	-	2	

Sew Borders

Sew 1½" S1 to 2½" S2. Press toward S2
Sew 1½" S2 to 2½" S1. Press toward S2

Measure star section to figure border length.

Stars Length _____ + 3¼" = _____ Length of Long Border

Stars Width _____ + 3¼" = _____ Length of Short Border

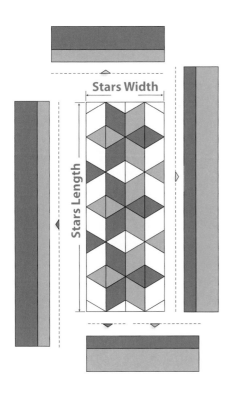

Cut (1) **long** border of each border strip.

Cut (1) **short** border of each border strip.

Using a partial seam on the first border, sew on the borders. Follow the diagram beginning with the partial red seam. Then sew the long red seam, followed by yellow, then green.

Quilt as shown in the illustration below or consider other options pictured throughout the book.

New Quilter? Anita hand quilted in the pattern shown. The different colors give a guide on how to make the fewest starts and stops for either hand or machine quilting. In the borders, to keep the quilting continuous where the lines end at the edge, "travel" between the points. To travel when hand quilting, run the needle between the layers without making any stitches. When machine quilting, "travel" by stitching in the ditch along the seam (the side without seams underneath).

Congratulations! You've just pieced your first stars!

Galaxy of Stars

80" x 97"

Pieced & Quilted by Marci Baker

Key to symbols:
FW: Full Width of fabric
1/2W: Half Width
1/4W: Quarter Width

Recommended Tools:
8" Clearview Triangle (Minimum)

I have found that I see inspiration in many unexpected places. The inspiration for this quilt came from three cups sitting on my kitchen counter when I was at home with two toddlers. My sons are now in high school and I am finally publishing this design! The photo of the tumblers shows the vivid colors that I needed to gather. As for the final design, I had no true idea of what would happen, but I wanted a stream of stars that resembled the Milky Way. Over a few months' time I collected the violets, golds, and pinks. The original selection of pinks was too cool and didn't fit with the violets. Once I found these warmer ones, I was ready to cut into the fabrics.

As you step through this project, I will explain different design elements that happened by planning and some that were serendipitous. Having a basic idea and letting it simmer with time is one of my favorite parts of the quilting process. I look at the final project and am amazed at the twists and turns that create the wonderful ending. I have had several projects that were rushed to be finished. More often than not, they have a forced quality that does not offer the full potential of the piece. That is why it has taken so many years to put this design onto paper. Now is the time for you to share in the process!

As mentioned, selecting the fabrics took some time. Keep swatches of your selected fabrics with you so when you have an opportunity to pick more, you have the others to compare. The nice part of this design is that most of the fabrics are only ¼ yard. You can collect more and then pull out the ones you do not want to use. Having a good range of values is important. Finding the darkest and lightest of the range can help define which others you need. One part of the design happened when I had already made the stars and was laying out the "galaxy". I found that I needed to remove two star sets which also included one of the gold and one pink. These matched most closely to the cups as can be seen in the photo, which took me by surprise. By having this gap in the range, the line of the stars appeared. I recommend that you work with a full range of colors, and make all of the star combinations. When you are laying out the stars and contrast fabric, you can then decide which part of your stars will define the galaxy. Another point when selecting the different ranges: notice that the darkest background (yellows) is significantly lighter than the darkest stars (purples) and darkest contrast (pinks). You need to have the contrast in value to allow the star designs to shine through.

Fabric Yardage				
S Stars	Bk Stars Background	C Contrast	BB* Border Background	Backing
(16) ¼ yd ea.	(8) ⅜ yd ea.	(8) ½ yd ea.	5 ¼ yd	8 ¼ yd

*This includes 1 yd for binding.

Cut Strips

Cut the strips as follows:

Size	S	Stars Bk
2½" x FW	16 total	8 total
2" x FW	32 total	16 total

Cut all of these strips into 1/4W.

When I am designing a quilt, I like to use smaller amounts of more fabrics. To allow for this variety and keep the strip-piecing method, I often work with strips that are half or one-fourth of the width of the fabric. These strips can vary in length and that is fine because the variation is cut off with the cut of the first angle.

Sew Strip-Sets

Each star has three different star fabrics and one background fabric. To create the shading across the quilt, make 16 star sets so that no two groups are repeated. Select S1, S2, S3, and Bk for each star set. To achieve the look of the original quilt, do not let the range of the star fabrics get too far apart.

For each star set, with 2 ½" strips in the middle and 2" strips on both sides, sew strip-sets as shown in the diagram. Sets should measure 5 ½" across. Be as consistent as possible and the pieces will work.

2" Star Sets: 1/4W of 16 combinations

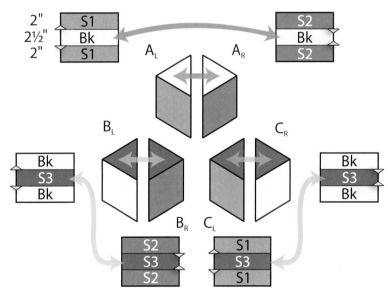

Cut Shapes

Cut 2" half-blocks of quantity shown in diagram using instructions for left on page 108 and for right on page 109.

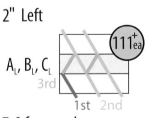

2" Left

A_L, B_L, C_L

3rd

1st   2nd

7-8 from each combination

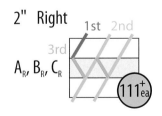

2" Right

1st   2nd

3rd

A_R, B_R, C_R

7-8 from each combination

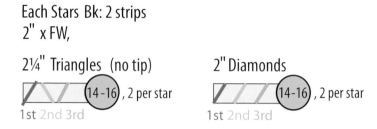

Want a Tip? A faster way to cut these is to pair them by A, B, or C. Place wrong sides together and use the cutting instructions for whichever is on top.

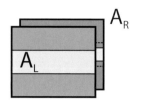

Cut the following shapes from the strips indicated in the diagram. If more information is needed see pages 111 - 112.

Each Stars Bk: 2 strips
2" x FW,

2¼" Triangles (no tip)   2" Diamonds

(14 -16) , 2 per star   (14-16) , 2 per star

1st 2nd 3rd   1st 2nd 3rd

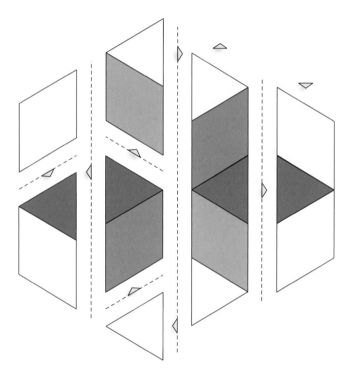

Sew Blocks

Lay out the left and right half-blocks into stars as shown in the diagram. Place background pieces at edges as shown. Sew the pieces into strips and sew strips together in pairs, pressing away from center, see pages 115 - 117 if more detail is needed. Join pairs to complete each block, press center seam either direction.

Layout

If you prefer to cut the outermost border with lengthwise grain, cut lengths of border background slightly longer than the quilt and the width of strip listed in border section before cutting the following. Cut the shapes of contrast and border background as needed for your particular layout. For more detail, see pages 111 & 114.

Each Contrast: 2-3 strips   BB: 26 strips
3½" x FW   3½" x FW

3¾" Triangles (no tip)   3¾" Triangles (no tip)   3¾" Half-Triangles
                                                          (half L, half R)

(40⁺) , 360 Total   (478)   (56)

1st 2nd 3rd   1st 2nd 3rd   1st 2nd 3rd

Lay out the stars and setting pieces in the desired design. Use the photo as a guide on layout and shading. Note that the stars can be rotated rather than keeping seams running a particular direction. Once you have decided on the final layout, I suggest taking a picture so that you can refer to it later.

Piece together and press seams as follows:

• Sew triangles onto opposite sides of the hexagon, being consistent with the position of the two triangles. Press toward triangles.

• At the top and bottom, piece and press seams of the first row of triangles, right to left for the top and left to right for the bottom. This will allow seams to match with the next border of triangles.

• On the sides, piece the border background triangles into half-hexagons.

Sew these star/triangle units together into rows across the quilt. Sew the rows together. Square up the center unit keeping ¼" seam allowance.

Want a Tip? Visit our website to download yardage and instructions for this smaller version of Galaxy of Stars: www.online-quilting.com/book-addenda/index.html

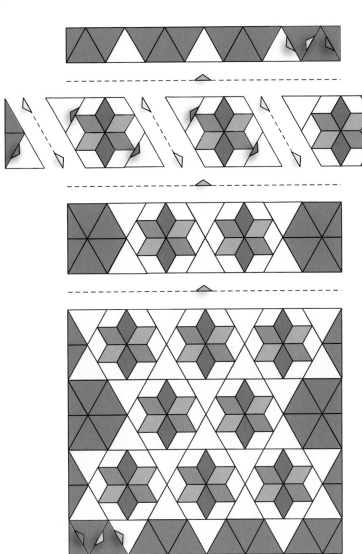

Sample is 3 stars x 5 stars
Quilt is 9 stars x 13 stars

Borders

There are two pieced borders of triangles. Sew and press seams as shown in the diagram, for the inner border clockwise, and for the outer border counter-clockwise. This will give seams that oppose and match easily. Piece the inside border to the outside border for each of the four sides.

To fit your pieced borders to your pieced center, you need to measure your quilt top and borders, compare the finished sizes, and determine if a fill strip is needed and what size to make it. Have the top and borders well pressed but not stretched.

Point-to-Point

Border sample is 9 x 12 contrast triangles
Quilt is 21 x 26

Use the following chart to help with these numbers.

1. Measure the quilt top through the center, top to bottom and side to side, in a couple of places. Subtract seam allowance for finished size of quilt top. Make note of these measurements.

	Finished Width of Center Width - ½"	Finished Length of Center Length - ½"	Top / Bottom Borders Point-to-Point	Side Borders Point-to-Point
My Measurements	_____	_____	_____	_____
Designed Size	65 ¾"	84"	72 ¾"	90"

2. Measure top/bottom borders and note average size from triangle corner to triangle corner as shown in diagram. (This is finished size, so do not subtract seam allowance.) Measure the side borders and note average size from triangle corner to triangle corner.

3. For a perfect fit, the top/bottom borders should measure 6" longer than the quilt top is wide. As shown in the table above, the difference is closer to 7". To allow for this 1" difference, a ½" finished fill strip was added to both sides of the center, to make it wide enough to fit the top/bottom borders. This requires (5) 1" strips of border background.

4. The side borders should measure 6" longer than the length of the center. If this measurement is less than ¾" difference from the 6", ease the variance as the borders are sewn to the center. If it is more than ¾" insert strips as done above.

Cut, measure and sew (11) 3½" borders strips together to make strips that are approximately 6" longer than pieced borders, or use lengthwise-grain strips cut previously on page 56. Sew these outer strips to each of the four pieced borders, being sure the strip is on the correct side. Apply the borders with mitered corners which are at 45° angles. See page 119 for details on mitering borders.

Backing, Quilting, and Binding

Use the following measurements to prepare backing and binding. For detailed instructions on each of these steps, see pages 120 - 126.

Size	Binding	Backing
Your favorite size, pg 123	12	(3) 2¾ yd

For a quilting design, I started near the center of the galaxy (of the quilt) and quilted lines that divided the top into sections (red). I call this method "divide and conquer" which makes machine quilting easier because I am working with only small amounts at a time. This swirl pattern is shown here. Between the lines of the swirl, I made a serpentine line extending the length of the band (yellow). Then on each side of the serpentine line, I filled in the space with a variety of sizes of small swirls. This is one of my favorite designs to quilt, where the line circles in to a center point (red), then does an abrupt change back out of the circle and on to the next center point (yellow and then green). Try this quilt design here or on your next project to add curve and motion with the quilting. Now you can say "Oh, My Stars!"

Heaven Can Wait 48" x 60"

Pieced by Brenda Backx ✷ Quilted by Alicia Sanchez & Marci Baker

Photographed Quilt is: 62" x 67"

Key to symbols:
FW: Full Width of fabric
1/2W: Half Width

Recommended Tools:
8" Clearview Triangle (Minimum)

Who has not been touched by the fear and sadness of breast cancer experienced through a friend or family member? As a way to support breast cancer awareness, Northcott Fabrics has produced many designs for The Quest for a Cure™ campaign. A portion of the sales from each yard sold from these fabric collections is donated to that cause. A few words including "friends", "hope", and "love", meander through the Baby Blocks and Stars pattern across the entire quilt. These are truly encouraging thoughts to everyone that a cure will be found.

Many corporations, charities, and fundraiser groups have joined in the fight for a cure through donations directed toward research and treatment. A simple search on the internet will result in a vast amount of information regarding breast cancer, including shops and online catalogs where you can purchase fabric lines related to breast cancer awareness. Look for the pink ribbon – the symbol for breast cancer awareness. Make a quilt to support this cause and make heaven wait for those dealing with breast cancer.

Note that the values in the diagram are placed differently than the quilt. For the photographed quilt, the dark is in the position of the light and would require the amount of fabric needed for the light. Also, this yardage is for a quilt that finishes to 48" x 60", rather than the size shown.

Fabric Yardage*

S Star	L Light Block	M Medium Block	D Dark Block	Border 1	Border 2	Backing
(3) ½ yd ea.	¾ yd	½ yd	½ yd	⅜ yd	2 yd	3 yd

* This yardage is for a 48" x 60" quilt, not the photo size.

Cut Strips

Cut the strips as follows:

Size	S	L	M	D
2½" x FW	2 of ea.	6	-	-
2" x FW	4 of ea.	-	6	6

Cut these strips into 1/2W as needed to make the strip-sets as shown in the diagram. Note that some strip-sets can be sewn as FW with pressing opposite directions at each end. I prefer to work in shorter lengths and stay organized by having everything grouped, so I cut everything to 1/2W.

Sew Strip-Sets

With 2½" strips in the middle and 2" strips on both sides, sew the strip-sets as shown in the diagram. Strip-sets should measure 5½" across. Be as consistent as possible and the pieces will work.

Want a Tip? Yes, we do want to sew the same fabric back together. The seam defines the diamond and looks best when included.

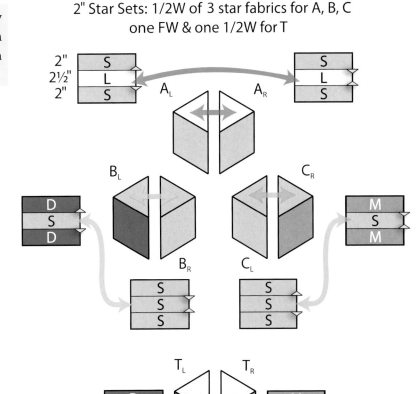

2" Star Sets: 1/2W of 3 star fabrics for A, B, C
one FW & one 1/2W for T

Cut Shapes

Cut 2" half-blocks of quantity shown in the diagram from each strip-set following the instructions for left on page 108 and for right on page 109.

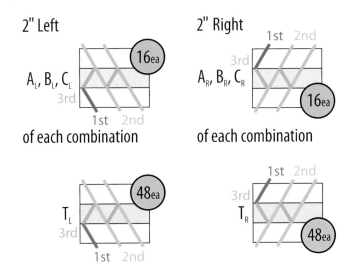

2" Left

A_L, B_L, C_L 16ea
of each combination

T_L 48ea

2" Right

A_R, B_R, C_R 16ea
of each combination

T_R 48ea

Cut the following shapes from the strips indicated in the diagram. If more information is needed see page 111.

L: 1 strip
2" x FW

2¼" Triangles (no tip)

1st 2nd 3rd ⟶ (24)

Layout

Lay out the left and right half-blocks into the stars outlined in red using the diagram. The sample is 3 stars x 4 stars, whereas the full design is 6 stars x 8 stars. (The photo is 6 stars x 9 stars.) You can place the various stars in the pattern shown, in diagonal rows, or any other design you like. Place block halves in-between stars as shown outlined in yellow. To fill in along bottom, use light triangles outlined in green. Sew the pieces into long strips, pressing seams according to diagram. Sew strips together in pairs, pages 115 - 117. Join to complete the top. Straighten the edges by trimming just past the star points, leaving ¼" seam allowace.

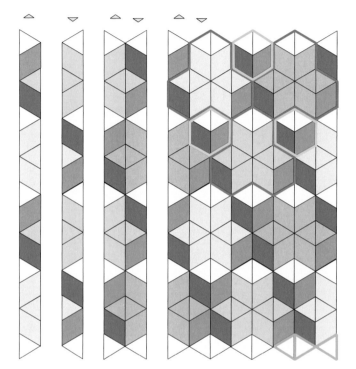

Borders, Backing, Quilting, and Binding

Use the following measurements to add borders and to prepare backing and binding. For detailed instructions on each of these steps, see pages 118 - 126.

Size	Border 1	Border 2	Binding	Backing
1½" x FW	5	-	-	(2) 1½ yd
6" x FW	-	5	-	
Your favorite size, pg 123	-	-	6	

This design is shown so you can see just the outline of the stars, just the stars, and the combination. For the outline, begin at the open circle and follow red, yellow, green, repeated until the solid circle. This pattern can be repeated across any size quilt. Notice only two lines of stitches are needed to outline one row of stars.

Quilt as shown in the illustration or consider other options pictured throughout the book. Follow the red, yellow, then green for continuous quilting.

Want a Tip? For the star, divide the "flower" by stitching figure 8's
rather than single petals in a clockwise fashion. My experience shows
the figure 8's turn out smoother and more even.

My Hero

73" x 79"

Pieced & Quilted by Leoba Weishaar

Lee refers to this quilt as "My Hero" because she has dedicated it to her husband who served 27 years as a firefighter before retiring. She is especially proud of the duties he performed as an arson investigator and chief of fire prevention. And by making this quilt she also fulfilled her desire to give a heartfelt tribute to those who risked their lives coming to the aid of the 9/11 victims. The postage stamp fabric itself is very moving in its depiction of the loyalty and dedication given by all those heroes during that tragic event.

Her inspiration to make this quilt was born from seeing a version of Seven Sisters that my staff had made for a kit, along with the idea that she wanted to make a special quilt for her husband. As a result, she purchased the red, white and blue postage stamp fabric and created her own version of the "Heroes" quilt.

Fabric Yardage				
S* Stars	Bk* Background	F* Focus Stamps	Binding	Backing
(4) 1¼ yd ea.	2 yd	2¾ yd	¾ yd	5 yd

* This includes enough for all 6 borders, including lengthwise cuts for outermost border only.

Cut Strips

This quilt requires 2FW star sets, one of reds and one of blues. Cut the strips as follows:

Size	S	Bk
2½" x FW	2 of ea.	4
2" x FW	4 of ea.	8

Sew Strip-Sets

Group the two star sets as shown in the diagram.

With 2½" strips in the middle and 2" strips on both sides, sew the strip-sets as shown in the diagram. The strip-sets should measure 5½" across, but the method is flexible. Be as consistent as possible and the pieces will work.

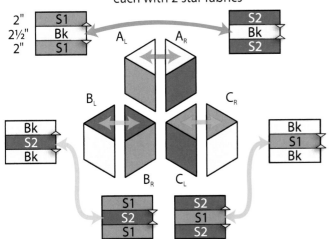

2" Star Sets: 1 FW each of 2 combinations each with 2 star fabrics

Cut Shapes

Cut 2" half-blocks of quantity shown in the diagram from each strip-set following the instructions for left on page 108 and for right on page 109.

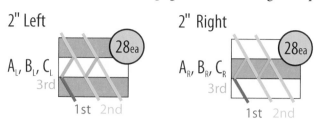

Cut the following shapes from the strips indicated in the diagram. If more information is needed see pages 111 - 112.

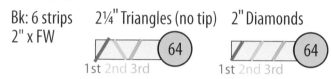

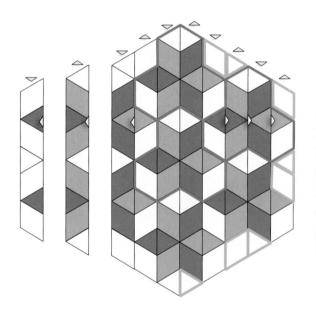

Sew Blocks

Lay out the left and right half-blocks into the Seven Sisters blocks using the diagram. Notice how four blocks have a blue star in the middle and four have red. Place background pieces at edges as shown. Sew the pieces into long strips, alternating the direction of pressing seams. Sew strips together in pairs. Join pairs to complete each block. See pages 115 - 117 if more detail is needed.

Seven Heroes   55" x 61"
Pieced by Mary Harpold ✶ Quilted by Marci Baker

Layout

When I designed this quilt, I made it so that I put the most number of blocks in the quilt. Later Mary Harpold, a friend of mine, pieced this other layout. I really liked the opportunity to place a secondary star design around the center hexagon and included it in Seven Batik Sisters, see page 71. Consider either one as a setting option.

If wanted, cut lengthwise borders using measurements on page 70 and label as borders for later use.

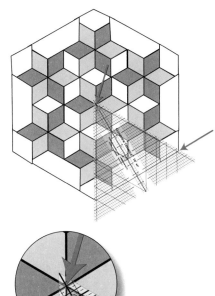

Prior to cutting the setting pieces, measure your blocks and make adjustments if needed as follows. First, measure the setting triangle size by placing the ruler as shown in the diagram. The ¼" seam allowance lines on the ruler are aligned with the pieced seams of the stars and the top point of the seam lines matches the center of the block. Read the measurement from the ruler, along the outside edge of the block. This is the triangle size and should be 8¼". Make note of yours in the table below.

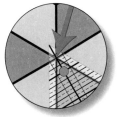

Shape	Design Size	My Size
Triangle	8¼"	_____
Half-Block	9¼" x 15½"	_____

Second, measure the size of rectangle needed for the half-block shapes. Fold a block in half matching bottom point to top point. Measure from the point to the fold and add ¼". This should be 9¼". Measure the block side to side. This should be 15½". Note your size of rectangle for half-block setting pieces in the table above.

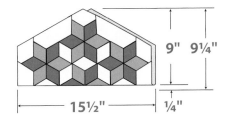

Before cutting all of the strips and shapes in the diagram, I recommend that you cut one of each shape first and make sure it matches your blocks.

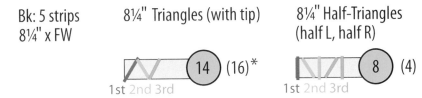

Bk: 5 strips 8¼" x FW

8¼" Triangles (with tip) 14 (16)*
1st 2nd 3rd

8¼" Half-Triangles (half L, half R) 8 (4)
1st 2nd 3rd

*Number needed for alternate setting is in parentheses.

For the half-block, cut a rectangle of background fabric, either 9¼" x 15½" or use your adjusted numbers. Fold the rectangle in half side to side (widthwise). Align edge of ruler along fold and point of ruler at top of fold. Cut along top edge of ruler.

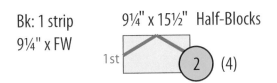

Bk: 1 strip 9¼" x FW

9¼" x 15½" Half-Blocks 2 (4)
1st

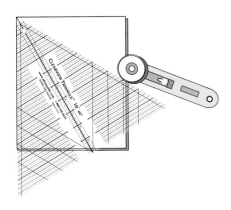

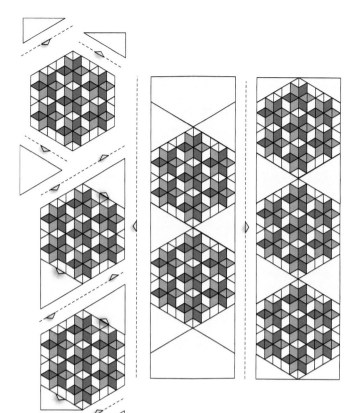

Lay out the blocks and setting pieces as shown in the diagram. Join triangles and half-triangles to blocks and half-blocks to make diamonds. Then sew into rows and finally rows together as shown. Press as indicated.

Borders, Backing, Quilting, and Binding

Use the following measurements to add borders and to prepare backing and binding. For general instructions on each of these steps, including mitering, see pages 118 - 126.

Size	2 med S	2 dark S	Bk	F	Binding	Backing
1¾" x FW	9 ea.	-	-	-	-	(2) 1½ yd
2½" x FW	-	9 ea	9	-	-	
6½" x FW	-	-	-	9	-	
Your favorite size, pg 123	-	-	-	-	9	

For this quilt there are 6 different borders. When there are this many, it is easiest to sew the border strips together and apply the border as one unit with mitered corners. This is why there are as many strips of the first border as the last border.

Join strips to create two of each star fabric, background, and contrast in the lengths of 80" and 90". Sew strips together into two 80" borders and two 90" borders. Measure, mark, pin, and sew the borders to the center unit, mitering at the corners. For more information on mitering see page 119.

Quilt the stars as shown in the illustration or consider other options pictured throughout the book. Start at the red circle, follow the line to the arrow, then continue with yellow and green. Repeat the pattern starting the second red circle to get the final design as shown.

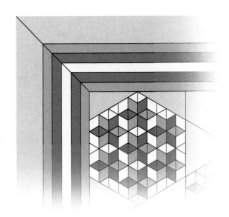

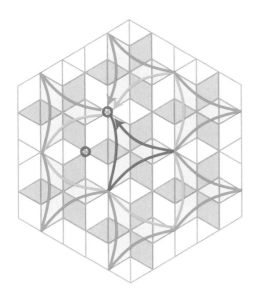
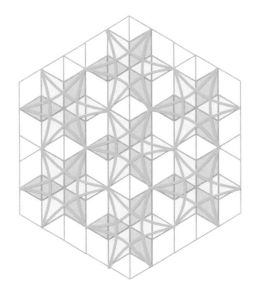

Seven Batik Sisters - 61" x 68"
Pieced by Jenny Hubbard ✳ Quilted by Marci Baker

My Sister's Tote

15" x 17"

Pieced & Quilted by Marci Baker

In 1995, while working with 60° diamonds, I sketched this "new" design and titled it Firework. In researching the background of different designs for this book, I found the same "old" design titled Columbia Star. This goes to show that nothing is new, except what you bring to creating this tote. Instead of making a typical tote, I thought "out of the square box" and created a unique bag sewn in a hexagon shape with a star in the center. This shape allows plenty of room to hold your quilt projects, use as a handbag, or carry traveling items. The batik fabrics I used resulted in a very striking bag, but depending upon the colors you choose this tote can be used for almost any occasion.

Fabric Yardage

S Star	Bk Background	C Contrast	Boxing Strip	Binding	Lining
½ yd	½ yd	½ yd	½ yd	½ yd	1½ yd

Cut Strips

Cut the strips as follows:

Size	S		Bk	C
3 ½" x FW	1		1	1
3" x FW	2		3	2

Cut all of these strips into 1/2W.

Sew Strip-Sets

With 3 ½" strips in the middle and 3" strips on both sides, sew strip-sets as shown in the diagram. For this design, both left and right halves are cut from the same set.

Find the center point of the sets and snip the seam allowance. Press one end with seams in, the other end with seams out. Sets should measure 8 ½" across. Be as consistent as possible and the pieces will work.

Want a Tip? Yes, we do want to sew the same fabric back together. The seam defines the diamond and looks best when included.

3" Star Set: 1/2W

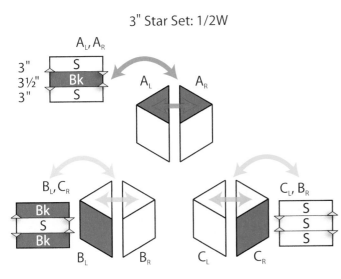

The contrast pieces around the star are made in the same manner. Sew the strip-sets D, E, and F shown in the diagram and press as described above with one end seams in, and the other end, seams out.

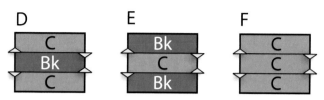

Cut Shapes

Left and right half-blocks, 3″ size, are cut simultaneously from each strip-set. Fold the strip-set in half, wrong sides together, locking/matching the seams. Cut the number of half-blocks shown in the diagram. Follow directions for the side that is right side up (on top), either left with the seams pressed out, page 108, or right with the seams pressed in, page 109. Because this is a tight fit, start the cutting at the fold end and trim off the least possible.

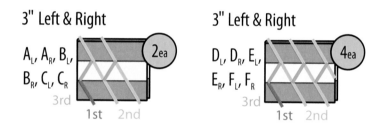

For edge pieces, cut the following shapes from the strips indicated in the diagram. If more information is needed see page 111.

Bk: 1 strip
3″ x FW

3¼″ Triangles (no tip)

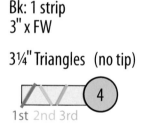

Layout

Make two blocks as shown in the diagram, using left and right half-blocks. Lay out the contrast pieces around the star. Use triangles to fill in at the top. Remove the contrast triangle from the half-block at the top as shown to fill in the triangle at the bottom. Another option would be to cut these triangles from another 3" contrast strip.

Sew pieces together into long strips alternating the direction seams are pressed. Sew strips together in pairs and join pairs to complete each block. See pages 115 - 117 if more detail is needed.

Trim ¼" beyond points to complete the hexagonal block.

Constructing the Tote

From background fabric cut the following pieces. If you desire, piece the boxing strip from remaining half-blocks with strips along sides for an added design element.

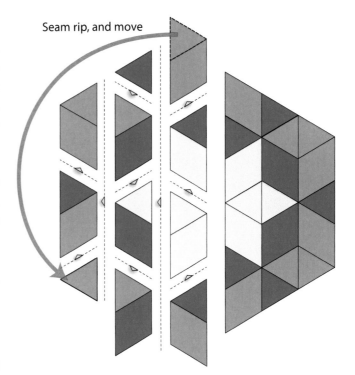

Seam rip, and move

Size	Shape	Bk	Binding	Lining
5" x 28½"	boxing strip	1	-	1½ yd
8" x FW	12⅛" trapezoid, gusset	2	-	
2½" x FW	-	-	3	

With right sides together, attach a gusset to each end of the boxing strip with ¼" seam.

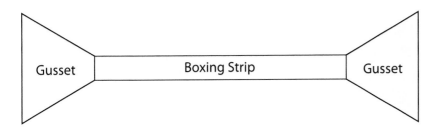

Gusset | Boxing Strip | Gusset

Layer the boxing strip and hexagon blocks with one large piece of batting and the lining. For batting we recommend Quilter's Dream Cotton, supreme or deluxe weight, which are thicker and provide more stability than thinner batting. Quilt as shown in the illustration at left or consider other options pictured throughout the book.

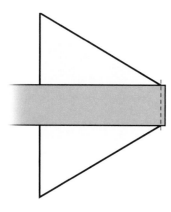

Cut out the quilted pieces. With lining sides out, fold the boxing strip at each end just below where the gusset attaches. Sew a ⅛″ seam to create a rib, as shown.

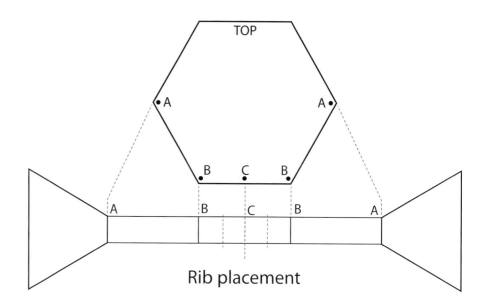

Rib placement

From these first ribs, mark the points that match your block's corner points (¼″ in from edge). See Diagram. Fold at each point with lining side out, and make a rib. If the strip is too long, add more ribs in center to give more stability to the bottom of the bag.

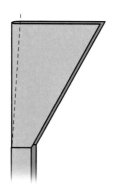

With lining side out, fold each gusset in half and take a scant ¼″ seam in from the fold, tapering like a dart just above the boxing strip reducing the stitch length at the end to secure the seam.

With lining sides together, sew the hexagons on both sides of the boxing strip and gussets, matching the ribs at the side and bottom corners. Fold the ribs down at the sides and in toward center at the bottom. If needed, you can trim out some of the rib and/or batting at these points.

Apply binding to the edges of hexagons, leaving the top unfinished for now. See the basic binding instructions for how to miter these angles, page 124. Finish by hand or machine as desired.

Want a Tip? Using two layers of scrap batting and lining, test the binding strip size for machine finishing. On the back (boxing strip side) apply the binding with ¼″ seam allowance, and then turn to the front. From the front, sew with a decorative stitch to catch the edge.

There are many options available for handles, including webbing, fabric, and pre-made. This tote has webbing. Another option would be to make fabric handles from quilted fabric or fabric covered cording. (Use a stretch stitch or shorter stitch length so that the stress of the bag does not break the stitching of the handle.) For another tote, we chose to purchase a set of faux leather handles and attach them with a fabric loop at the top edge. See below.

To attach the handles:

1. Align raw end of handles/loops with raw edge of top of tote, on the inside, near the corners. Baste in place.

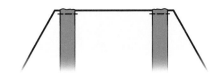

2. Trim remaining binding strips to 2¼"

3a. If loops are being used, apply the binding to the inside of the tote over the loops. Slide handle rings onto loops and fold loops around with raw edge aligned with outside edge of tote (like a belt loop). Finish applying binding to outside edge, machine stitching over the loop. (Be sure purchased handles are attached correctly prior to sewing.)

3b. For fabric handles, like the webbing, apply the binding to the inside of the tote over the handles. When folding binding around to finish outside edge, have handles folded up and catch in machine stitching for binding. Reinforce at these points with smaller stitches or two rows of stitching.

Designing Quilter? Put more stars in your bag as Alicia did here. Make two Seven Sisters blocks from a 2" star set that is 1/2W in length. Cut the strips listed here and follow instructions in My Hero for Seven Sisters layout.

(1) 2½" S
(2) 2" S
(1) 2½" Bk
(1) 2" Bk

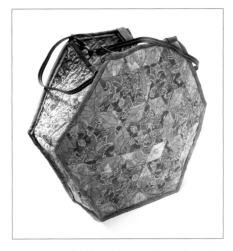

Pieced & Quilted by Alicia Sanchez 15" x 17"

2" Star Set: 1/2W

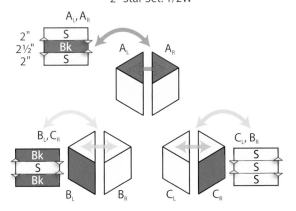

O' Christmas Tree

30" x 31"

Pieced & Quilted by Kerry Ayers Cain

Key to symbols:
FW: Full Width of fabric (~ 40")
1/2W: Half Width (~ 20")

Recommended Tools:
8" Clearview Triangle (Minimum)

What a joyful little quilt to hang on the wall at Christmas time! This was made by Kerry, who was taking a class from me. We collaborated on layout options, and what began as a few star blocks became an endearing tree. The pyramid of stars reaches toward the sky with its spiked greenery. In keeping with this festive season, Kerry used red fabric for the background, sprinkled stars throughout, and then adorned the tree with dangling miniature Christmas lights and stitched a gold garland. So, what comes next? Presents, of course! She placed gifts under the tree that are just waiting to be opened on Christmas Day. You can add your own touch by "wrapping" the presents with various fabric prints and attaching ornaments and garland to your heart's content.

Fabric Yardage

S1 Star 1	S2 Star 2	Bk Background	Border 1*	Border 2	Binding	Backing
⅜ yd	⅜ yd	1 yd	¼ yd	⅝ yd	⅜ yd	1¼ yd

*If using lamé, I recommend applying it to a fusible stabilizer before cutting to minimize raveling. Also note the required fabric care for cleaning.

Cut Strips

Cut the strips as follows:

Size	S1	S2	Bk
2½" x FW	1	1	1
2" x FW	2	2	3

Cut all of these strips into 1/2W.

Sew Strip-Sets

With 2½" strips in the middle and 2" strips on both sides, sew the strip-sets as shown in the diagram. Strip-sets should measure 5½" across, but the method is flexible. Be consistent as possible and the pieces will work. Make a note of your measurement.

2" Star Set: 1/2W

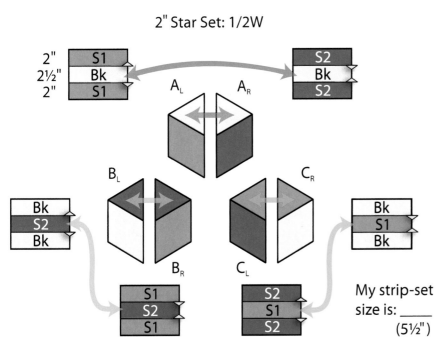

My strip-set size is: _____
(5½")

Cut Shapes

Cut 2" half-blocks of the quantity shown in the diagram using instructions on page 108 for left and page 109 for right.

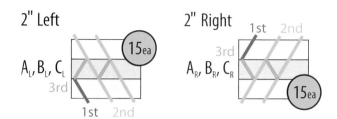

Cut the following shapes from the strips indicated in the diagram. Use your strip-set if it is ⅛" or more different than 5½". If more information is needed see pages 111 - 113.

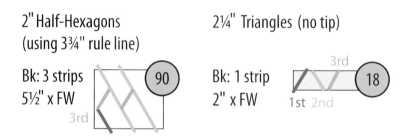

> **Want a Tip?** When piecing an overall design, consistent sewing works great. So when designing with large background areas, I still piece this. That way, it adds a texture and lines for quilting it later, and the top will lay flatter because it is sewn consistently throughout. To be sure the cut pieces match the sewn pieces, measure your strip-set width and cut using that as a template.

Layout

Layout the pieces following the diagram turned sideways for correct orientation of the stars relative to blocks A, B, and C. Sew the pieces into long strips and sew strips together in pairs, pages 115 - 117. Join to complete the top. Square by trimming ¼" past the star points.

Appliqué the tree trunk (2 ⅜" x 4 ½"), the star, and packages (2" x 2", 3" x 3 ½", or similar size) using your favorite appliqué method, see page 127 for appliqué references.

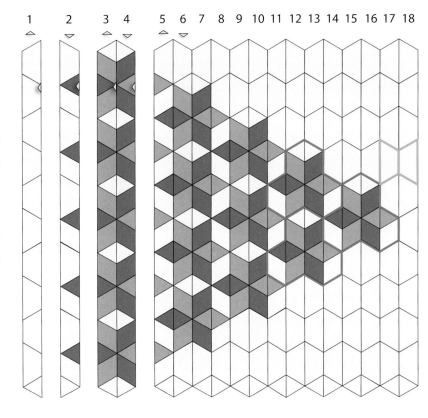

**Actual Size Star
for O'Christmas Tree**

Borders, Backing, Quilting, and Binding

Use the following measurements to add borders and to prepare backing and binding. For detailed instructions on each of these steps, see pages 118 - 126.

Size	Inner Border	Outer Border	Binding	Backing
1¼" *	4	-	-	(1) 1¼ yd
3½"	-	4	-	
Your favorite size, pg 123	-	-	4	

*or 1" folded in half, added to inside edge of outer border for a flange.

Quilt as shown in the photo with metallic threads, or consider other options pictured throughout the book. This is a great project size for practicing machine quilting.

Designing Quilter?　For the candy cane stripe effect, cut the binding on bias. Here is an easy way to fold the fabric especially when binding fabric is not a square. Fold up so raw edges match at left and/or fold is on bias. Fold again so folds are parallel to each other and to ruler lines. To reduce the number of seams, start by cutting near the center and cut strips from each of these sides until there is enough for the project. Join strips as usual, crossing at any angle, sewing from key point to key point in a straight line.

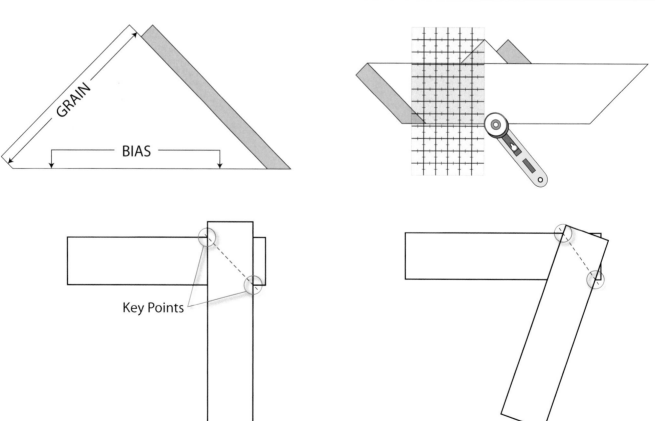

GRAIN

BIAS

Key Points

Pretty in Pink 45" x 54"

Pieced by Janice Schlieker ✷ Quilted by Marci Baker

Here is a fast and easy quilt to make. Its charming simplicity inspired Janice to use this pattern for a special friend. The user-friendly instructions are written for extra large stars, which lets you stitch it up in no time! Janice pieced this top in just 5 hours. This quilt is made with bright and cheerful fabrics, but any color way is sure to please anyone and everyone on your list.

Fabric Yardage			
S Star	Bk Background	Binding	Backing
1 yd	1 ½ yd	½ yd	2 ¾ yd

For the background pick a value significantly different than the star fabrics. This contrast will make the stars appear more obvious!

Cut Strips

Cut the strips as follows:

Size	S	Bk
4 ½" x FW	2 of ea.	3
4" x FW	4 of ea.	6

Cut all of these strips into 1/4W.

4" Star Set: FW of 3 combinations

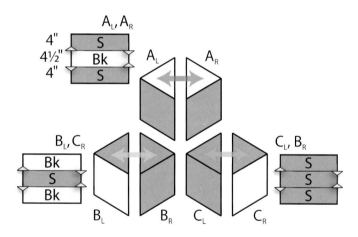

Sew Strip-Sets

With 4 ½" strips in the middle and 4" strips on both sides, sew the strip-sets as shown in the diagram with the right sides together using a scant ¼" seam. Label according to left or right halves of block A, B, or C. Press in the direction of the arrows. Sets should measure 11 ½" across. Be as consistent as possible and the pieces will work.

Want a Tip? Yes, we do want to sew the same fabric back together. The seam defines the diamond and looks best when included.

PRETTY IN PINK

Cut Shapes

Left and right half-blocks, 4" size, are cut simultaneously from each set. Fold the set in half, wrong sides together, locking/matching the seams. Follow directions for the side that is right side up (on top), either left with the seams pressed out, page 108, or right with the seams pressed in, page 109. Because this is a tight fit, start the cutting at the fold end and trim off the least possible.

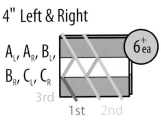

Layout

Lay out the left and right half-blocks into the stars using the diagram. You can lay them out in the diagonal form or mix it up. Fill edges with remaining parts of stars. Sew the pieces into long strips and sew strips together in pairs, pages 115 - 117. Join to complete the top. Square the top by trimming ¼" past the star points.

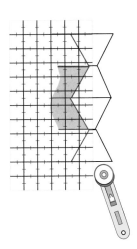

Backing, Quilting, and Binding

Use the following measurements to prepare backing and binding. For detailed instructions on each of these steps, see pages 120 - 126.

Size	Binding	Backing
Your favorite size, pg 123	5	(2) 1⅜ yd

Quilt as shown in the illustration or consider other options pictured throughout the book. Note how the butterfly design has lines that "hit" center points on the diamond edges at the black dots. When making a design, I use center points, ends of pieced lines, and other consistent points to define the design. Then as I am free-handing the quilt design, I aim for those points trying to keep the curves as smooth as possible. Another trick that I used on this quilt was to practice on the busier fabrics and those with less contrast to the quilting thread. Then by the time I got to the third butterfly on the dark pink, I had a fairly smooth and flowing rhythm to my quilting.

Star of David   *23" x 20"*

Pieced & Quilted by Marci Baker

Key to symbols:
FW: Full Width of fabric (~40")
1/2W: Half Width (~20")
1/3W: Third Width (~13")
2/3W: Two-Thirds Width (~26")

Recommended Tools:
8" Clearview Triangle (Minimum)

In today's society, the Star of David is commonly accepted as the Jewish symbol. The symbol can be found on menorahs, dreidels, jewelry, and challah covers. Challah is the braided bread used for Jewish festivals and the Sabbath. I designed this cover at the request of Rabbi Elisheva Salamo of the San Francisco Jewish Community Center for a quilting class. The center star is a Traditional Star of David. The outer stars represent the 12 tribes of Israel. The inner star piecing method is based on Sara Nephew's designs in *Big Book of Building Block Quilts* and *Not Your Grandmother's Log Cabin*™.

Fabric Yardage for Center Star of David			
S* Star	Bk1 - Blue Background	Bk2 - Gold Background	A* Accent
¼ yd	½ yd	¼ yd	⅛ yd

*This includes enough for borders.

Fabric Yardage for 12 Tribes of Israel Stars			
S1 Star1	S2 Star 2	Bk3 Background	Backing
⅜ yd	⅜ yd	½ yd	⅞ yd

When making this quilt, it is very important that you are sewing with a scant ¼" seam allowance. See page 14. If more than ¼" is removed from the front of the design, the outer stars will not fit the inner star. Pressing is also important for this to fit.

Center Star of David

Cut Strips

Cut the strips as follows:

Size	S	Bk1	Bk2	A
3 ¼" x FW	-	-	1	-
3" x FW	-	1	-	-
1" x FW	3	-	-	2

Only two-thirds of the length of these strips is used. If desired, cut these to 28"- 30" lengths.

Sew Strip-Sets

With the 3" Bk1 in the middle and 1" star, S, on each side, sew the strip-sets as shown in the diagram. Press one seam toward star and one seam toward background. The accent strip is pieced as a flange. Press 1" accent strips in half wrong sides together lengthwise. With raw edges matched, sew accent, A, on each side of 3 ¼" Bk2.

Strip-Sets: 2/3W or FW

1"S		1"A folded
3"Bk1		3¼" Bk2
1"S		1"A folded

Cut Shapes

From the S-Bk1-S strip-set, cut (3) 3 ¼" diamonds and (3) 2 ¾" diamonds (Will *not* be 2 ¾" on all sides). Then cut each diamond into two triangles of corresponding size. There will be a strip of scrap fabric left over from each diamond. See page 111.

2¾" & 3¼" Triangles (w/tip)   3¼" Triangles (w/tip)

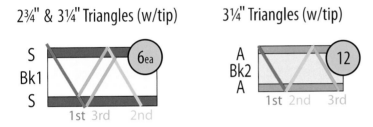

From the A-Bk2-A strip-set, cut the following triangles. There will be a tip of contrast that needs to be pulled off.

From the remaining S strip, cut the following trapezoids. See page 112.

3¼" Trapezoids   (Flat-pyramids)

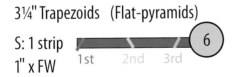

S: 1 strip
1" x FW   1st   2nd   3rd   6

Sew Block

For less chance of dark shadowing through on the 2 ¾" S-Bk1 triangles, press seam toward dark. Sew trapezoids on left side of 2 ¾" S-Bk1 triangles. Press toward dark.

Make 6 wedges as shown in diagram matching the pieces that have the same pressing directions. Press as noted.

Alternating direction of top seam, lay out wedges into the Star of David. Sew and press each half (set of 3) in clockwise order. **Leave as halves.**

Leave as halves

12 Tribes of Israel Stars

Cut Strips

Cut the strips as follows:

Size	S1	S2	Bk3
2 ¼" x FW	1	1	1
1 ¾" x FW	2	2	4

Cut all of these strips into 1/2W.

1¾" Star Set: 1/2W

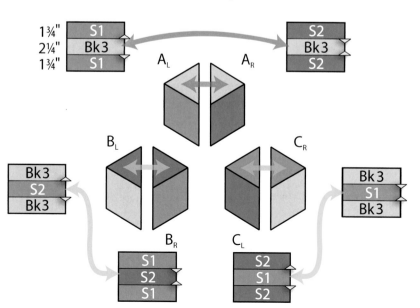

Sew Strip-Sets

With 2 ¼" strips in the middle and 1 ¾" strips on both sides, sew the strip-sets as shown in the diagram. Strip-sets need to measure 4 ¾" across.

Cut Shapes

Cut 1¾" half-blocks of quantity shown in diagram using instructions for left on page 108 and for right on page 109.

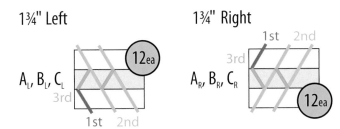

Cut the following shapes from the strips indicated in the diagram. If more information is needed see pages 111 - 112.

Bk3: 3 strips, 1¾" x FW

Layout

Lay out the design following the diagram. Sew pieces together in long strips using pages 115 - 117. for guidance on the type of seam. Press seams according to diagram. Sew strips together into pairs, then into units. Sew units together for the finished top.

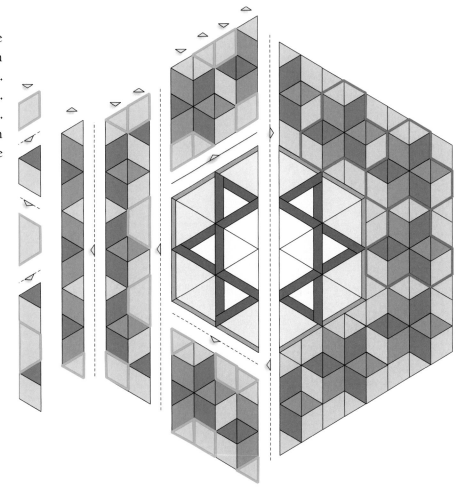

Borders, Backing, and Finishing

Use the following measurements to add borders and to prepare backing. For detailed instructions on each of these steps, see pages 118 - 126.

Size	Border	Accent Border	Backing
1"	-	2	(1) ⅞ yd
2"	2	-	

Again, the accent is pieced in as a flange. Press 1" accent strips in half wrong sides together lengthwise. With raw edges matched, sew one accent strip on one side of each 2" border strip.

Fold and cut these into 1/3W strips, approximately 14". Attach each border to each side stopping the seam at ¼" points at both ends. Miter the borders at each corner, see page 119 for details, if needed.

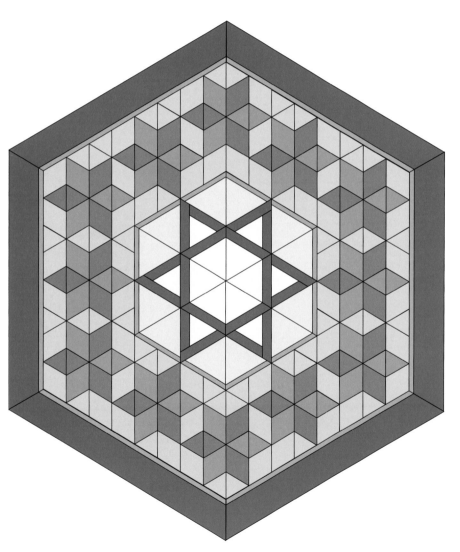

For the challah cover I didn't want the stiffness of a quilted item. So I placed the top and the backing right sides together and stitched around all edges, leaving 4 - 5" unstitched for turning. Then I trimmed the corners to reduce the bulk, turned and hand-stitched the edge closed. To keep the layers together, I stitched in the ditch through the two layers, just around the Star of David. Enjoy making your Challah cover part of your family tradition!

Stars & Stripes

52" x 49"

Pieced by Anita Hartinger ★ Quilted by Marci Baker

STARS & STRIPES

Quilt made by Mary Rockhold Teter, 1861. Photo courtesy National Museum of American History, Smithsonian Institution.

. . . forever! In fact, stars and stripes have been incorporated into American flags since the late 1770s. Many renditions of the flag were made during those early American years. While Betsy Ross was one of many people to sew a flag, her design was one of the most famous from that era. In 1861, Mary Rockhold Teter of Noblesville, Indiana, created a quilt in honor of her son while he was serving in the Civil War, shown here. She appliquéd 34 stars in the center and in the border to represent the number of states that were in the Union at that time. She also stitched not only her son's name but also included names such as "Ab" and "Abe Lyncoln", among other words. She was inspired to make this quilt based upon a design in an 1861 issue of a women's periodical, *Peterson's Magazine* of Philadelphia.

As quoted from her 1897 obituary, *"She was of a family of strong, patriotic Revolutionary stock . . . Her grandfather was Capt. John Rockhold . . . who served in the War for Independence. . . . Her father, Joseph Rockhold, . . . was a captain in the War of 1812. This trait of patriotism was one of the strongest in the character of Mrs. Teter. During the late war she showed her great love for the soldier boys in many ways, aiding in every way she could to encourage and help in the country's peril."* Her Stars and Stripes quilt was obviously considered a dear heirloom as it stayed in the family's possession until it was donated to the Smithsonian Institution in 1940.

The attraction and uniqueness of this early American quilt was so strong, it inspired Anita to create her own version of it. While the quilt may appear to be a project for an experienced quilter, this is Anita's second quilt! As proven here, the rotary cutting techniques, the sewing tools, and the strip-piecing methods which I teach open up opportunities to quilters of all skill levels that would otherwise be daunting.

Fabric Yardage

S Star	Bk Star Background	R* Red Stripes	W* White Stripes	Binding	Backing
1½ yd	1½ yd	1¼ yd	¾ yd	½ yd	3¼ yd

*If you buy red-and-white striped fabric (average 1¼" wide stripes) you'll need 1½ yds total.

Want a Tip? Consider piecing the borders first to gain confidence in cutting and sewing the stars while working with larger pieces.

Designing Quilter? Consider representing the 13 colonies in the stars in the medallion by selecting a second star color, like gold. You will need ½ yd of this second color. Watch for Designing Quilter steps throughout the project for this variation.

Center Medallion

Cut Strips

Cut the strips as follows:

Size	S	Star Bk
2" x FW	4	2
1½" x FW	8	4

Sew Strip-Sets

With 2" strips in the middle and 1½" strips on both sides, sew the strip-sets as shown in the diagram. Strip-sets should measure 4" across, but the method is flexible. Be as consistent as possible and the pieces will work.

Want a Tip? Yes, we do want to sew the same fabric back together. The seam defines the diamond and looks best when included.

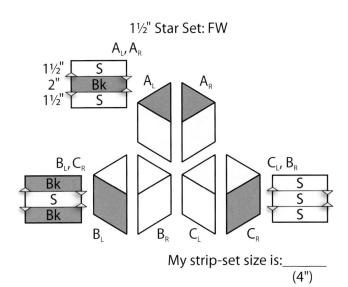

1½" Star Set: FW

My strip-set size is:_____
(4")

Designing Quilter? If using a second star color for the 13 colonies, then cut half of the star strips from each color. Cut all strips to half-width. Make one half-width star set for the main star color and one half-width star set for the second star color. Depending on the width of the fabrics, you may need to sew an additional quarter width star set for the main star color.

Cut Shapes

Cut 1½" half-blocks of quantity shown in the diagram from each strip-set following the instructions for left on page 108 and for right on page 109.

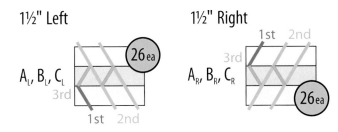

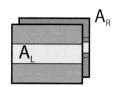

Designing Quilter? Cut 13 of each half-block for main star color and 13 of each half-block for second star color.

Cut the following shapes from the strips indicated in the diagram. Use your strip-set size if it is ⅛" or more different than 4". If more information is needed see pages 111 - 113.

Bk: 2 strips, 1½" x FW

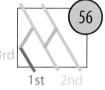

1¾" Triangles (no tip)   1½" Diamonds   1½" Half-Hexagons (using 2¾" rule line)

14   16   56

1st 2nd 3rd   1st 2nd 3rd   2 strips 4" x FW   3rd   1st 2nd

Medallion Layout

Lay out the left and right half-blocks into the stars using the diagram. Fill in sides with cut background shapes. Sew the pieces into long strips, pressing seams as noted. See pages 115 - 117 for more detail if needed. Sew strips together in pairs. Join to complete the medallion.

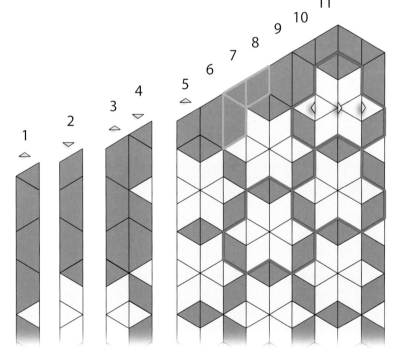

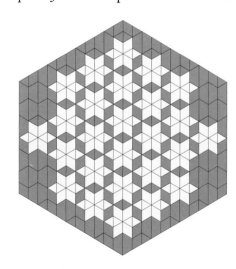

Border Stars

Cut Strips

Cut the strips as follows:

Size	S		Star Bk
2½" x FW	4		2
2" x FW	8		4

Sew Strip-Sets

With 2 ½" strips in the middle and 2" strips on both sides, sew the strip-sets as shown in the diagram. Strip-sets should measure 5 ½" across but the method is flexible. Be as consistent as possible and the pieces will work.

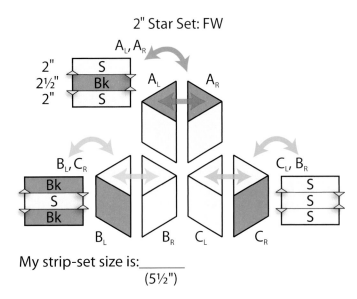

2" Star Set: FW

My strip-set size is:_____
(5½")

Cut Half-Blocks

Cut 2" half-blocks of quantity shown in the diagram following the instructions for left on page 108, right on page 109.

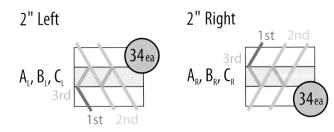

2" Left   2" Right

A_L, B_L, C_L A_R, B_R, C_R

34ea   34ea

Cut the following shapes from the strips indicated in the diagram. Use your strip-set size if it is ⅛" or more different than 5 ½". If more information is needed see pages 112 - 113.

2" Half-Hexagons (using 3¾" rule line)

Bk: 3 strips
5½" x FW

82

STARS & STRIPES

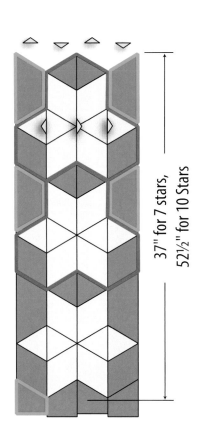

37" for 7 stars, 52½" for 10 Stars

Sew Borders

For the borders, lay out two borders with 7 stars and two borders with 10 stars, filling in edges and ends with the half-hexagons as shown in the sample 3-star layout diagram. Sew each border into 4 rows each, alternating pressing direction, and joining rows into final borders. Ends are trimmed after making the center section, to allow for adjustments.

Center Stripes

For the center stripes cut the following strips:

Size	R	W
3" x FW	2	-
2" x FW	13	-
1½" x FW	-	14

With 3" red strips on outer edges, sew strips together. Press all seams toward red. This should measure 39" by the fabric width.

Want a Tip? To avoid a skewed center panel, sew strips in pairs and alternate the direction of the seams, starting at the opposite end when the pairs are sewn together. If one of the strips is longer than the other, adjust so one end aligns almost straight and any extra is all at one end.

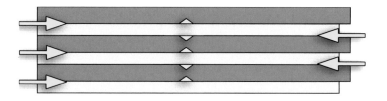

Measure the 7-star borders including seam allowance past the star points. Note the average length, should be about 37". Measure the 10-star borders also, making note of average length, which should be about 52 ½". Using these measurements, cut the center panel of striped fabric to a length of the 10-star border minus 12", which should be 40 ½". Cut the width to 37" or your adjusted measurement, trimming equal amounts from both outer red stripes. Trim excess off border ends as needed. See diagram.

Want a Tip? While working with these long pieced bias borders, you may find some are longer than others by ½"more. To release any stretching which may have occurred while pressing, lay the borders flat and spritz with water. This allows the fabric to draw up to its original size. Let it air dry and with a gentle hand, press again. Now measure to see if they are closer in length.

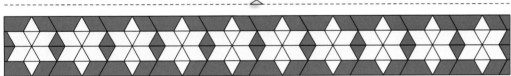

Add the borders to the center panel, as shown in diagram.

Appliqué the medallion with your favorite method to the striped panel using center points to align the piecework.

New Quilter? To avoid the red stripes shadowing through, sew the medallion right sides together with a piece of muslin, leaving a hole for turning. Turn right side out, stitch opening closed, and appliqué in place.

Borders, Backing, Quilting, and Binding

Use the following measurements to prepare backing and binding. For detailed instructions on each of these steps, see pages 118 - 126.

Size	Binding	Backing
2" x FW	6	(2) 1⅝ yd

Quilt as shown in the illustration or consider other options pictured throughout the book.

Stars Over Colorado *76" x 50"*

Pieced & Quilted by Shirley Gisi

Designer Section

For the designing quilter, I have included information that is useful when creating your own star quilt. You can use it to figure finished sizes and yardages. Consider sharing your design on our website to inspire even more quilters to make their own.

Stars Over Colorado by Shirley Gisi is an example of what can be done with this technique. Though she made the stars with traditional methods, the layout and ideas can be implemented more easily with the strip-piecing method. I generally design where I have at least 3 to 4 stars of the same colorway to make good use of the overhead in strip piecing. If I only need 1 or 2 stars, I would consider cutting individual triangles and diamonds to create the half-blocks for that particular star, which is how Scott Hansen made his stars in City Lights.

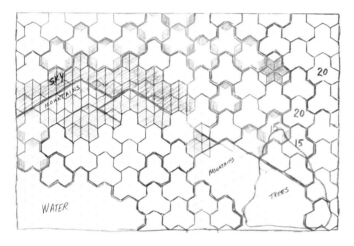

There are many ways to divide up Shirley's design, and I have considered several. However, I have always come back to working these designs as the basics of 3 blocks, because it always works. There are several places where the design can have variety, but one pair of strips must always match. In a star set the middle strip fabric has to be used both in a left strip-set and in a right strip-set to make the horizontal diamonds. However, the outer strips can be different and are a great opportunity for using more variety in the fabrics. Working with shorter pieces is another way. As can be seen in designs such as Galaxy of Stars and All Stars, I work with 1/4W strips. Only with the smaller stars as in City Lights does 1/8W strips make sense to allow more variety.

I often begin a design on graph paper with colored pencils. Outlining the stars/blocks makes it easier to determine the piecing strategy.

Another way that I work is to collect fabric for the project, cut one of each size strip, make the combinations, and see what comes together. This is how the Galaxy of Stars was designed. I had 7 to 9 fabrics of each of the color ways and made some basic decisions about which would be stars and background and started making combinations. Only when I had the stars in individual blocks was I able to bring the idea to a reality.

Here are some of the numbers to keep in mind when making your own design. I have offered the sizes of the stars used throughout the book. However, any size can also be done, like the size in My Sister's Tote. I wanted the single star block to match the size of the Seven Sisters design for the other tote. So there was a need for the 1 ¾" star set. For any size, the middle strip is ½" wider than the outer strip and half-blocks are cut the same width as the outer strips.

Star Measurements

This table gives finished size and cut size for the different stars in the book.
Refer to the diagram for understanding the measurements.

	Size of Star Set (S)	1½"	1¾"	2"	2½"	3"	3½"	4"
Finished	Triangle Height (TH = S - ½")	1	1¼	1½	2	2½	3	3½
	Triangle Width (TW = TH/0.866)	1⅛	1½	1¾	2¼ +	2⅞	3½	4
	Star Height (3 x TW)	3⅜	4⅜	5¼	7	8⅝	10½	12
	Star Width (4 x TH)	4	5	6	8	10	12	14
	Block Height (4 x TW)	4½	5¾	7	9¼	11½	14	16
	Overlap (TH)	1	1¼	1½	2	2½	3	3½
	Star Width - Overlap (3 x TH)	3	3¾	4½	6	7½	9	10½
Unfinished	Outer Strip Width (S)	1½	1¾	2	2½	3	3½	4
	Middle Strip Width (S + ½")	2	2¼	2½	3	3½	4	4½
	Triangle Height (S + ¼")*	1¾	2	2¼	2¾	3¼	3¾	4¼
	Diamond Height (S)	1½	1¾	2	2½	3	3½	4
	Half-Block Width (S) (from strip-set)	1½	1¾	2	2½	3	3½	4
	Half-Hexagon Rule Line	2¾	3¼	3¾	4¾	5¾	6¾	7¾
	Setting Triangle Height (2 x TH + ¾")	2¾	3¼	3¾	4¾	5¾	6¾	7¾

*Cut from S (no tip) or S + 1/4" (with tip) strips

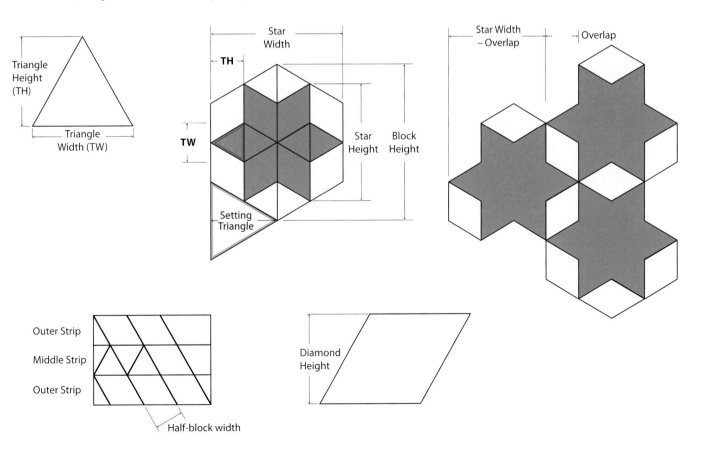

Yields

Use this table to determine how many pieces can be cut from a strip or strip-set. Use to find out how long of strips to cut for a particular design.

Shape	Length of Strips	Number of Pieces Per Strips/Strip-Set						
		Star Set Size						
		1½"	1¾"	2"	2½"	3"	3½"	4"
Triangle	40"	39	34	31	24	20	17	15
	20"	19	16	15	11	9	8	7
	10"	9	8	7	5	4	-	-
Diamond	40"	22	19	17	13	11	9	8
	20"	11	9	8	6	5	4	3
	10"	5	4	4	3	-	-	-
Half-Block	40"	44	38	34	26	20	18	16
	20"	20	18	16	12	10	8	6
	10"	10	8	6	4	4	4	-

Strip-Sets for Stars

Select the number of fabrics that will be used per star, then make the combination.

	A (top of star)		B (lower left of star)		C (lower right of star)	
	A_L	A_R	B_L	B_R	C_L	C_R
1 Fabric per Star	S1-Bk-S1	S1-Bk-S1	BK-S1-BK	S1-S1-S1	S1-S1-S1	Bk-S1-Bk
2 Fabrics per Star	S1-Bk-S1	S2-Bk-S2	Bk-S2-Bk	S1-S2-S1	S2-S1-S2	Bk-S1-Bk
3 Fabrics per Star	S1-Bk-S1	S2-Bk-S2	Bk-S3-Bk	S2-S3-S2	S1-S3-S1	Bk-S3-Bk
6 Fabrics per Star	S1-Bk-S1	S2-Bk-S2	Bk-S6-Bk	S5-S6-S5	S4-S3-S4	Bk-S3-Bk

Number of Strips for Star Set

Each strip-set has the middle strip which is wider (w) and two outer strips which are narrower (n). This table shows how many strips of each fabric of each width are needed for a particular Star Set.

	S1	S2	S3	S4	S5	S6
1 Fabric per Star	4w, 8n*	-	-	-	-	-
2 Fabrics per Star	2w, 4n	2w, 4n	-	-	-	-
3 Fabrics per Star	4n	4n	4w	-	-	-
6 Fabrics per Star	2n	2n	2w	2n	2n	2w

* w = wider middle strip; n = narrower outer strips

As an example of how to use the charts, let us look at Stars Over Colorado. Notice that there are four groups with 15-20 stars each. Find on the *Yields* chart a length for half-blocks that gives 8-10 pieces. The 1/2W of a 3" yields 10 half-blocks per strip-set. Therefore, this might be a good size to consider splitting each group into two. But how big will the final design be? There are 13 columns of stars across (which are staggered) and 7 ½ stars down. Looking at the *Star Measurements* chart, use the star height and width to determine finished size of the quilt. There is also overlap between rows of stars. This gives 13 x 7 ½ + 2 ½" = 100" for a finished width. And 7 ½ x 8 ⅝ x 2 ⅞" ≈ 65" for a finished height of the quilt.

If you have a smaller wallhanging in mind, notice that you can get eight 1¾" half-blocks from 1/4W strip-sets. Split the four groups into 3 each for 24 (need 20) and 2 each for 16 (need 15). The finished size on this will be 13 x 3¾ + 1 ¼" = 50" by 7 ½ x 4 ½ ≈ 34". This is a great size for a wallhanging and makes for using a variety of fabrics without a lot of extra stars.

Now look at the *Strip-Sets for Stars* table showing the different combinations to sew for the stars. We are using 1 fabric per star. Notice how the strip-sets are duplicated in the group. Many times I use this to my advantage and sew only three strip-sets that are twice as long as determined and cut both left and right halves from them at the same time as in Carolina Lily and My Sister's Tote. However, with this design more variation is better, so we make lefts and rights in shorter lengths from a larger variety of fabrics. For each star set we need 4 wide (4w) and 8 narrow (8n) of 1/4W strips of star fabric and 2w and 4n of 1/4W strips of background. Note that the wide strips always need to be in pairs because one is sewn for lefts and one is sewn for rights. Because of this, the top of a star A_L, A_R will have the same background fabric.

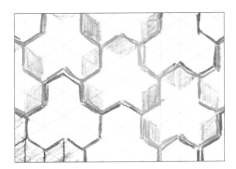

The outer strips for B_L and C_R block can be made using two different background strips each. For the orange outlines, some B_L and C_R will be light (pink) background and some will be medium (green) background as shown here.

To sum up the strips required, for each strip-set of a particular star set, cut (1) 2 ¼" and (2) 1¾" FW strips of the one star fabric and choose (1) 2 ¼"x 1/2W and (4) 1¾" 1/4W strips of background fabric. Cut all pieces into 1/4W to sew the star set, make 10 different star sets: 2 pink outline, 2 orange outline, 3 green outline, and 3 blue outline, with varying backgrounds as needed.

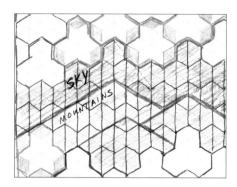

Shirley used large pieces of fabric to define each mountain. To make the piecing easier and more likely to lie flat, I would cut half-hexagons and triangles and diamonds from the particular fabric and position these to create the mountains. Having these pieced gives an overall grid for quilting purposes, too.

The drawback of many pieces however, is you can not use a particular fabric as effectively as Shirley's water fabric in the lower left hand corner. The other way to accomplish what she did is to appliqué the strip-pieced stars on top of the larger pieces.

Having the wide variety of techniques gives quilting today such an incredible potential – it is inspirational. Try different techniques and discover your favorite way to quilt.

Enjoy creating your own stars and sharing them with others. We would love to see what develops, so send pictures.

General Instructions

Left-Handed Cutting

Throughout this section the steps are illustrated as right-handed cuts. For left-handed quilters, turn the book upside down and follow the diagrams which are now left-handed cuts. I haven't changed the words for left-handed, but as most of my left-handed students tell me, they are used to reversing the process and the visual seems to be enough.

Want a Tip? I recommend using sticky notes or bookmarks to keep your place in this section and the project section.

Stars vary in size and different size rulers can be used. Note that the diagrams below may look slightly different than your actual pieces. What is important is that you align the highlighted ruler lines and make similarly angled cuts.

To keep my place when cutting, I use Qtools Cutting Edge™ which creates a physical stop on my ruler. The cuts are consistent in size and easy to align.

New Quilter? Left and right halves always have the triangle at the top. As you are cutting pieces, lay them out with the triangle at the top and the parallel sides at the sides.

Qtools Cutting Edge™

Cutting Half-Blocks

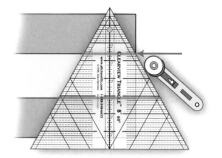

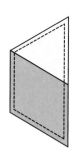

Left Half-Blocks (A_L, B_L, C_L)

Step 1.
Place triangle at right end of the strip-set with point up and ruler edge at right end of upper seam.

Match ruler lines with seams. Cut along right edge of the triangle.

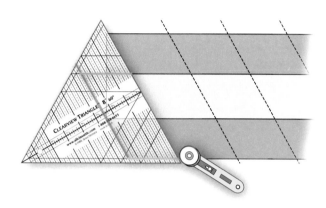

Step 2.
Turn strip-set with angled end to the left.

Cut slices the width of the size of the half-block by aligning the appropriate ruler line along the angled end and a horizontal line along the seam (best) or the strip-set edge. (ok).

After a few cuts, if ruler lines cannot be aligned to fabric, re-trim the angle as in Step 1. At the end of the strip-set, one more half-block can be cut, when the ruler is positioned for the next cut, if the top seam is at or extends beyond the edge of the ruler.

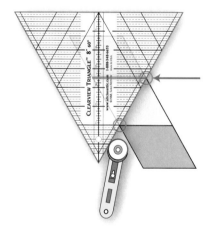

Step 3.
Cut slice into two left half-blocks as follows:
With slice "leaning" to the left, place any ruler line along upper seam.

Slide ruler along seam until ruler edge is at right end of seam. Ruler edge should also line up with left end of bottom seam. (If not, shift the ruler left or right to split the variance, while keeping the ruler aligned with upper seam.)

Cut and check with actual size drawing on page 110.

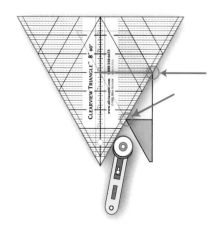

Right Half-Blocks (A$_R$, B$_R$, C$_R$)

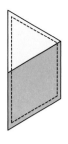

Step 1.

Place triangle at right end of strip-set with point down and ruler edge at right end of lower seam.

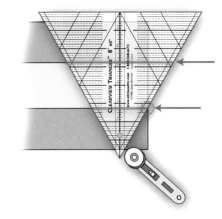

Match ruler lines with seams. Cut along right edge of the triangle.

Step 2.

Turn strip-set with angled end to the left.

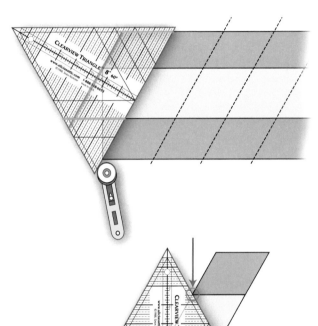

Cut slices the width of the size of the half-block by aligning the appropriate ruler line along the angled end and a horizontal line along the seam (best) or the strip-set edge (ok).

After a few cuts, if ruler lines cannot be aligned to fabric, re-trim the angle as in Step 1. At the end of the strip-set, one more half-block can be cut, when the ruler is positioned for the next cut, if the top seam is at or extends beyond the edge of the ruler.

Step 3.

Cut slice into two right half-blocks as follows:

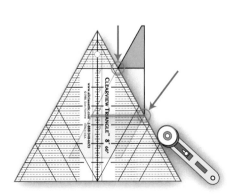

With slice "leaning" to the right, place any ruler line along lower seam.

Slide ruler along seam until ruler edge is at right end of seam. Ruler edge should also line up with left end of top seam. (If not, shift the ruler left or right to split the variance, while keeping the ruler aligned with lower seam.)

Cut and check with actual size drawing on page 110.

> **Want a Tip?** Once you have mastered cutting LH and RH, you can stack strips to cut them faster. With a left-half strip-set on top of and wrong sides together with a right-half strip-set, lock seams together so there are no gaps and no bulk where seams line up. Cut using the Left Half-Block cutting instructions, because left is right-side up in this stack.

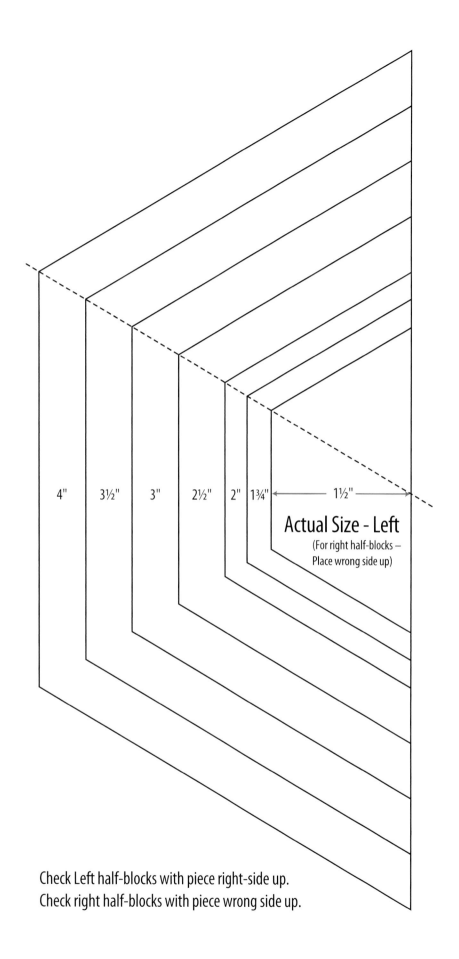

4" 3½" 3" 2½" 2" 1¾" ←————— 1½" —————→

Actual Size - Left
(For right half-blocks —
Place wrong side up)

Check Left half-blocks with piece right-side up.
Check right half-blocks with piece wrong side up.

Cutting Shapes

Here are some basic shapes which can be cut using the Clearview Triangle rulers. With each shape, the first cut is to make a 60° angle as shown here in **First Cut.** Cut shapes include seam allowances.

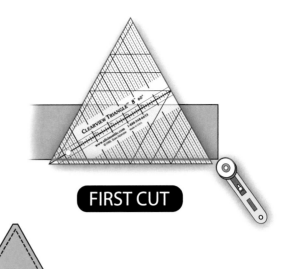

First Cut

At the right end of the strip, place the triangle with a point up and ¼" line aligned with lower edge of the strip. Cut along right edge of the triangle.

FIRST CUT

Triangles (no tip) (Total seam allowance is ½")

Most triangles for these projects are cut with tip missing to eliminate having another size of strip to cut. It is important to realize that **the measurement aligned on the ruler is the strip width plus ¼".**

Step 1.
Make cut as shown in **First Cut** above.

Step 2.
Turn strip with angled end to left.

With ruler point down and left edge of ruler at left end of strip, align the triangle size line (this is ¼" + Strip Width, e.g., 3¼" line aligned on 3" strip) along top of the strip. The tip of the triangle of fabric should be missing. Cut.

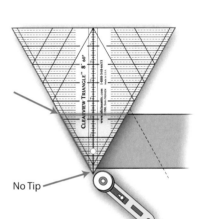

No Tip

Rotate the ruler and continue cutting triangles until you have the number needed for your project.

Triangles (with tip) (Total seam allowance is ¾")
For My Hero the 8¾" triangle is cut this way.

Step 1.
Make cut as shown in **First Cut** above.

Step 2.
Turn strip with angled end to left.

With ruler point down and left edge of ruler at left end of strip, align the triangle size line (this is same as the strip width e.g.: 3¼" triangle is shown) along top of the strip. The tip of the triangle of fabric is not missing. Cut. Rotate the ruler and continue cutting triangles until you have the number needed for your project.

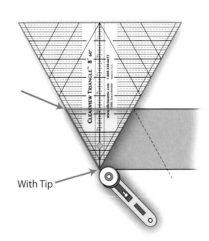

With Tip

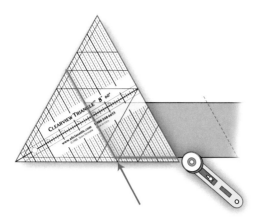

Diamonds (Total seam allowance is ½")

Step 1.
Make cut as shown in **First Cut** on page 111.

Step 2.
Turn the strip with angled end to left.

Place the triangle at left end with top point to the lower left. Align the appropriate rule line from the bottom of the ruler to cut the diamond at the same width as the strip. Example shows 3" diamond. Cut.

Continue cutting diamonds until you have the number needed for your project.

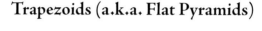

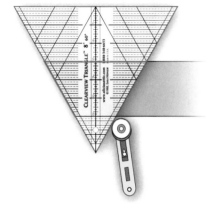

Trapezoids (a.k.a. Flat Pyramids)

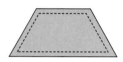

Step 1.
Make cut as shown in **First Cut** on page 111.

Step 2.
Turn the strip with angled end to the left. With the point of ruler down, align the trapezoid size line along the top edge of the strip and left edge of ruler along left edge of strip. Example shows 5" trapezoid. Cut.

Rotate the ruler and continue cutting trapezoids until you have the number needed for your project.

Half-Hexagons (Trapezoid on Bias)
This shape is cut to fill in around half-blocks and works well because it has the same grain as the half-blocks. If your seam allowance results in a significantly different (⅛" or more) strip-set size, cut your strip of fabric to match your strip-set size. Follow the instructions and modify as noted. Example shows 2½" half-hexagon from 7" strip.

Step 1.
Place triangle at right end of the strip with a point up and ¼" line aligned with lower edge of strip. To get the most out of the strip, slide the ruler sideways until the right edge is just above the center point of the end of the strip. This is approximate.

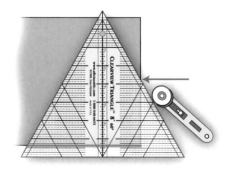

Step 2.

Turn the strip with angled end to the left. Cut slices the width of the size of the half-hexagon by aligning the appropriate ruler line along the angled end, and the ¼" line along the bottom edge of strip.

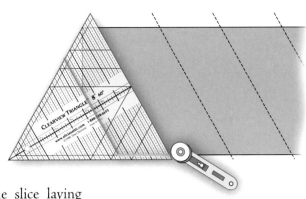

Step 3.

*(For a different strip size, see below.)

Cut the slice into two half-hexagons as follows. With the slice laying horizontal, align the rule line noted in your pattern along the bottom edge, and the left edge of the ruler along the left edge of the slice. Before cutting, check that the shape under the ruler and the shape not under the ruler are equal to your half-blocks.

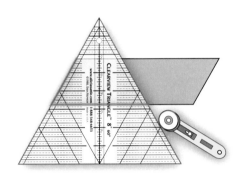

* If you used a different size strip to match your strip-set, use your half-block as a template to find the best rule line for your half-hexagons.

Want a Tip?   For any cut where the 60° ruler does not extend far enough, use 60° ruler and a long ruler together, then remove 60° ruler. To make a right-handed cut, position the ruler and strip based on the diagram upside down (a left-handed cut). Then put the longer ruler next to the triangle, remove the triangle, and make the cut.

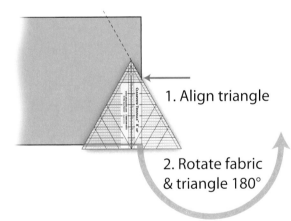

1. Align triangle

2. Rotate fabric & triangle 180°

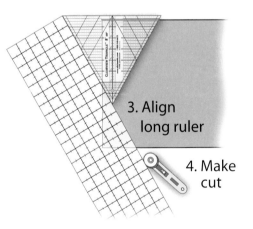

3. Align long ruler

4. Make cut

Half-Triangles (no tip)
(seam allowance is ½")

To cut the left and right at the same time, have two strips wrong sides together. Follow these instructions which are for left ones. For cutting only rights, follow the steps except in Step 2, have the ruler point down.

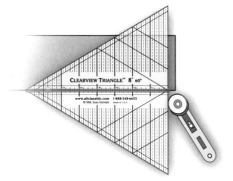

Step 1.
Align center line of ruler along bottom edge of the right end of the strip. Cut the end square.

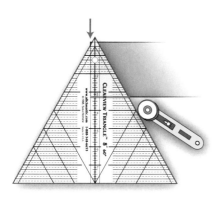

Step 2.
Turn the strip with cut end to the left. Align the quarter-inch line to the left of center line along left edge of fabric. Align size of half-triangle line along bottom fabric edge. The point of the ruler is ¼" above the edge. Make the cut.

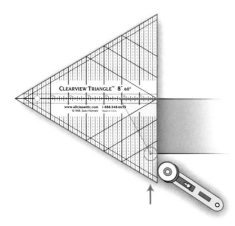

Step 3.
Align the center line of the ruler along the top edge of the strip and position the ruler so that ⅜" line is at the lower corner. Make the cut. Repeat second and third cuts as needed.

Sewing Pieces into Strips

When sewing the half-blocks together, quite often the seam has "ears". These are defined by where the edges cross each other (key points). By sliding the pieces back and forth, adjust the ears to fit your seam allowance. When the pieces are put into the machine, the needle should be at one key point and the seam end at the other.

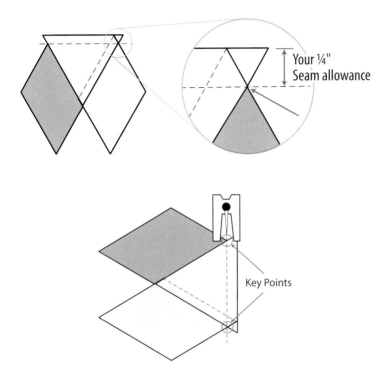

Your ¼"
Seam allowance

Key Points

If, after sewing the pieces together they are staggered as shown, then the ears are not matching your seam allowance and need to be adjusted. The pieces are sewn correctly if there is enough seam allowance at the point where the three pieces of fabric come together.

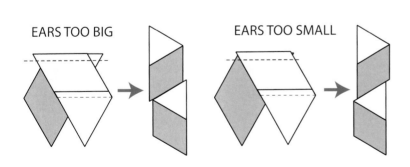

EARS TOO BIG

EARS TOO SMALL

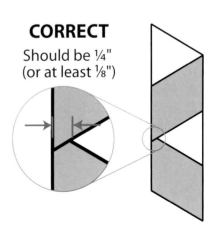

CORRECT
Should be ¼"
(or at least ⅛")

Another option for these seams is to use Qtools Corner Cut 60™ to trim the ears prior to sewing to match your seam allowance. Then the alignment and sewing at the machine are easier and faster.

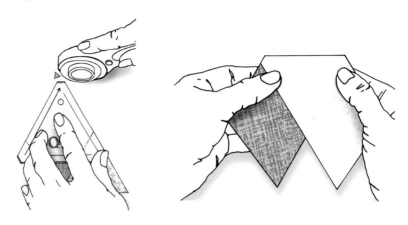

New Quilter? Here is a wonderful 'tool' that will save you thread, time, money, and frustration, and costs only a few fabric scraps!

Startie-Stoppies are pairs of layered fabric scraps (about 2" across) which are sewn in between continuous chain piecing. When you sit down to sew, sew across a Startie to the front edge. Now chain piece your strips, or half-blocks, or whatever you are sewing. When finished, chain piece and sew across a Stoppie to the front edge. Clip your chain piecing off at the back of the Stoppie. This Stoppie becomes the Startie for the next set of seams.

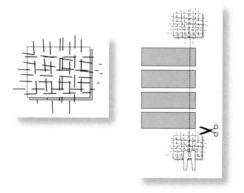

Here are just a few benefits from using these:

1. A Startie holds thread when starting to sew and feed dogs are less likely to feed on fabric edges.

2. Save thread – no long threads hanging. Also save time because there are no threads to clip off.

3. Hand turning the needle or lifting the presser foot are not required. (These will be the hardest habit to break).

The sooner you make using Startie-Stoppies a habit, the sooner you will be sewing like a pro!

As you sew the pieces together, pay extra attention to keep them in correct order. In many cases it is possible to position either way. Note that the diamonds are never sewn together.

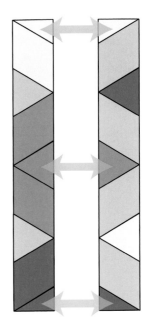

After each row is sewn, check that pieces are in correct order as planned. This is easily seen by noting whether triangles match each other to create the diamond.

For pressing the seams, the direction alternates between rows. **Do not change any previously pressed seams.**

Want a Tip? Since rows are pressed in alternating directions, press after all of the rows are sewn. Then pick up every other row and press in one direction. Pick up the other rows and press the opposite direction.

When pressing toward the top, hold top of row in left hand and press seams toward the top. If pressing toward the bottom, hold bottom of row in left hand and press toward the bottom.

Sew rows together in pairs.

Seams have been pressed so they lock together to match points. Use bias to ease between points. But be careful - it's bias! I lock the seams first without the strips being flat and then straighten the seam and ease as needed.

Where three seams are sewn together (six pieces of fabric), sew just outside the existing crossed seams (one thread's width) for perfect points. By starting half the seams at the bottom and the other from the top, you should be able to see these points each time.

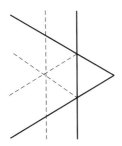

Trim pieced portion along edges as shown for quilt.

If you are not setting the blocks or attaching the borders right away, stay-stitch with machine, basting a scant ¼" away from edge to prevent stretching of bias edges.

Borders

New Quilter? Cut border strips either lengthwise or crosswise. If you are using a solid fabric it is best to cut lengthwise so there are no seams distracting from the overall design. If you are using a busier print fabric, you can cut crosswise and join the strips, but know that this direction is stretchier than the other and can cause rippling in the border if it is not measured and applied correctly.

For side borders, measure the length of the quilt in several places. Cut two strips of border to this measurement. Fold both border and top in fourths along edge. Mark quarter points by pinning or finger pressing. Pin the border to the quilt top with right sides together matching the quarter points. Sew. Press toward the border.

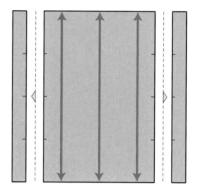

For top and bottom borders, measure the width of the quilt, including the side borders just added.

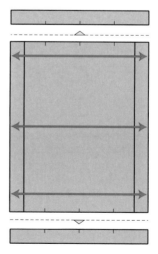

Cut, mark, sew, and press the top and bottom borders in the same manner as the side borders. This completes the first border. Repeat for any additional borders.

Mitered Borders

You can miter any angle of border using the following method. I learned this from my first quilting teacher as one of my first tricks that doesn't require a ruler. This method works best with at least 2" to 4" of extra length on each end of each border.

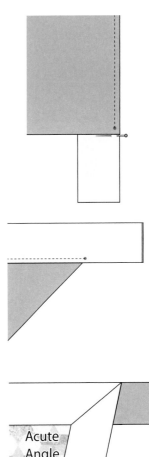

1. Measure borders as on previous page. Cut strips 4-8" longer. Mark with a pin where the borders match the edges of quilt top. Sew border strip on to each side, with stitching ending just before the point where ¼" seam allowances cross and pin is at edge of quilt top.

2. At each corner to be mitered, place borders right sides together starting at the inside corner and aligning edges. This will fold the quilt in half.

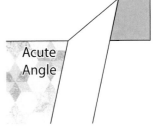

3. Keeping the borders together, unfold the quilt so it lays flat and the border folds along the miter to be sewn. Be sure the raw edges are still aligned. Press at this fold.

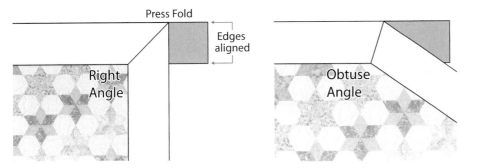

Right Angle

Press Fold

Edges aligned

Obtuse Angle

Acute Angle

4. Fold the quilt back as in Step 2 so that the wrong side of the pressed fold is visible. Pin the borders together. Stitch on the fold, starting at the ¼" point at the inside and ending at the edge.

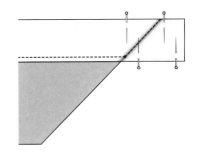

Want a Tip? One of my students said she uses this method, but uses double stick tape under the fold to hold the seam in place while sewing. This is an excellent idea . . . as long as I can find the double stick tape and I do not forget about it and iron the tape!

Quilting

Basting – Hand Quilting

Cut backing pieces and sew together as shown in the table for your quilt. This is about 3" larger than the quilt top, on each side. Using masking tape, attach the backing fabric to the floor or a table with right side down.

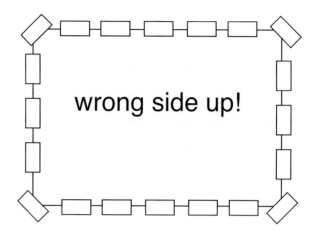

Cut the batting about 2" larger than the quilt top, on each side. Lay the batting on top of the backing, smoothing any wrinkles. Lay the quilt top, right side up, centering it on the backing.

To begin basting, take several overlapping stitches in different directions. This holds the thread tight enough without making big knots.

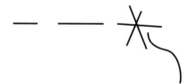

Hand baste with large running stitches through all three layers about every 3"- 4", following a grid pattern. Remove the tape. Fold the backing around to the front, covering the batting, and hand baste in place. This keeps the edges protected while quilting.

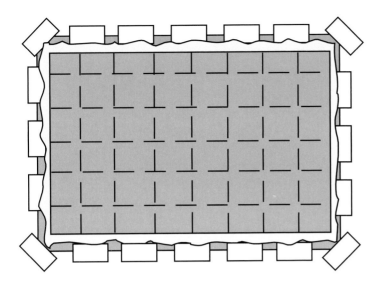

Basting – Machine Quilting

For machine quilting, follow the same instructions as above, but use safety pins to catch all three layers in a grid pattern about every 3"-4" apart.

If you decide to have the quilting done by a professional, do not baste the layers together. I recommend that you ask for references and look at samples of their work to know that they will add to your project the quality you expect.

The Quilting Stitch

Decide on the quilting design. For traditional hand quilting, a ¼" outline was often used. Other options for both hand and machine quilting are given for most projects.

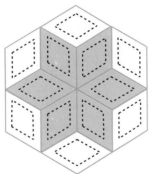

If marking the design, use pen, pencil, or chalk designed for marking fabric that can easily be erased or removed.

For details on machine quilting, see references listed on page 127.

For hand quilting, the stitch is a running stitch that goes up and down through all three layers. Hide knots in the batting layer by pulling gently through the quilt top.

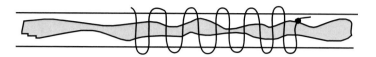

Use a quilter's knot to achieve a uniform knot that pulls through easily. Between needles (sizes 9-12) are best.

New Quilter? Thread the needle with 18"-24" of quilting thread. Place the end of the thread across the needle.

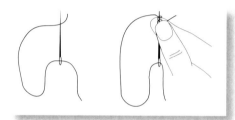 While holding it down between your thumb and forefinger, wrap the thread closest to the tip of the needle (but not the end) around the needle 2 or 3 times.

Holding the wrapped thread securely between your thumb and forefinger, pull the needle up until the length of thread has slipped through your fingers, leaving a consistently-sized knot at the end.

Binding

These binding instructions are for French binding, also called double binding. The binding is folded in half, sewn with a ¼" seam to the top, then wrapped to the back and hand stitched to the backing at the fold. (See cross-section diagram.) Instructions for standard ¼" binding, wide binding, and mitering different angles are shown.

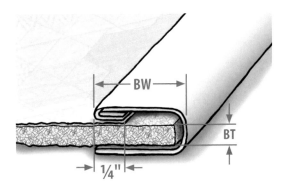

1. Trim and square quilt edges as necessary.

When possible, measure a specific distance from the seams in the quilt top. For example: Trim at 4 ¼" from seam if the last border is 4" finished with ¼" finished binding. Another example: Trim at 5" from seam if the last border is 4" finished with 1" finished binding.

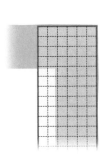 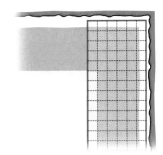

2. Cut strips for binding.

The width of the strip to cut (WS) depends on the finished width of the binding (BW) and the batting thickness (BT). Select your BW from the table. For BT of ¼", use the corresponding WS. For BT of ⅛", subtract ¼" from the WS. For BT of ⅜", add ¼" to the WS. Make adjustments if desired to find your personally perfect binding.

BW	⅛"	¼"	⅜"	½"	⅝"	¾"	1"	1 ¼"	1 ½"	2"
WS	1 ½"	2"	2 ½"	3"	3 ½"	4"	5"	6"	7"	9"

To find WS for a BW not listed, use the following: Add ¼" (for seam allowance) plus BW (for front) plus BT plus BW (for back). Multiply this by 2 (for double fold). In other words, WS=2 (1/4 + 2BW + BT).

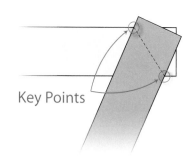

Key Points

Working with crosswise grain or bias grain (see page 82), cut enough strips for the perimeter of the quilt, plus 10"-12" extra.

3. Join the strips to make one long strip as follows:
With rights sides together, overlap two strips at any angle. Sew from where the strips cross (key point) on one side to where they cross on the other side in a straight line. Make sure both ends to be trimmed are on one side of the seam. If the strips are the same width and the seam is sewn straight from point to point, this makes one long straight strip. Trim excess to ¼" seam allowance. Press the seam open.

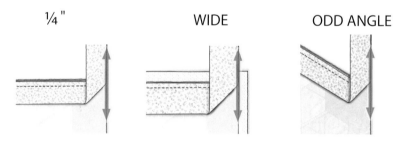

4. Fold binding in half and begin sewing in the middle of one edge of quilt. It is not necessary to press the fold. Align raw edges of the binding with raw edges of the quilt top. Leaving 10"-12" loose, and at ¼" in from edge, backstitch and sew the binding to quilt through all layers.

5. Sew to the corner, pivot, and sew to edge.
At the corner, stop ¼" away from both quilt edges with needle down in the fabric. Pivot and sew to the corner point and sew off the edge of the quilt. If not exactly at the pivot point, stop before it, not after.

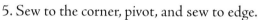

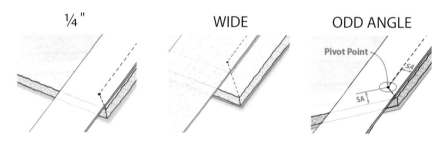

| ¼ " | WIDE | ODD ANGLE |

6. Fold binding along stitched line.
Turn the quilt to work on the next side. Fold the binding back along the angled seam line. Align the binding edges with the edge of the next side of the quilt top, making a straight line.

| ¼ " | WIDE | ODD ANGLE |

7. Fold the binding down with fold in line with the outer corner. Keep the binding edge and quilt top edge aligned.

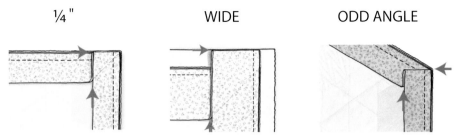

¼ "   WIDE   ODD ANGLE

8. Sew from the fold down to the next corner with a ¼" seam.

Continue binding and mitering each corner, stopping about 10"-12" (or more for wider binding) from the starting point. Backstitch and remove the quilt from the sewing machine.

9. Finish the binding by sewing the two ends together so the binding will lay flat as follows:

Unfold ends of binding. Lay each end flat along the quilt edge until they meet halfway.

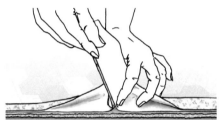

With ends right sides together, insert a pin ¼" in from the edge of the binding where the ends meet, the critical point (CP).

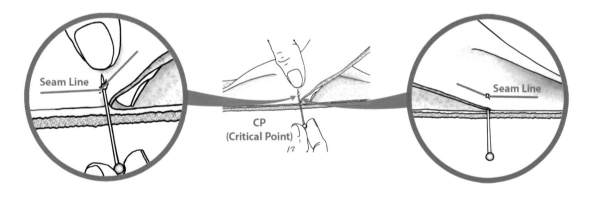

Seam Line

CP
(Critical Point)

Seam Line

Keeping only this point constant, rotate the binding ends so they lay across each other at an angle. Sew together with the seam described in Step 3, sewing through the CP. Once sewn, check that the binding lays flat along the quilt, then trim ends to ¼" seam allowance. Press the seam open.

Again, fold binding in half and finish sewing it to the quilt with a ¼" seam.

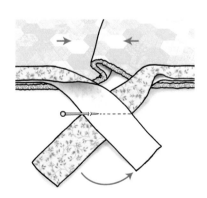

Want a Tip? View an online video of this method on our website, www.aliciasattic.com/video-tutorials-free/index.html

10. Fold the binding around to the back and hand stitch using a blind, ladder, or appliqué stitch.

At the corners, fold down the right side, then the left side to evenly distribute the bulk. Stitch down mitered corners on back and front, especially for wider bindings.

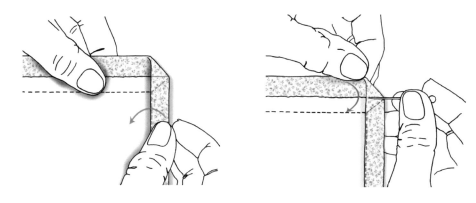

Want a Tip? For more detailed information on the do's and don'ts of binding, refer to the **Know Before You Sew**™ series. These are available at **www.aliciasattic.com.**

New Quilter? Now that you have finished your quilt, consider labeling it somehow. I use Pigma™ pens, which are fabric pens that can be set with heat. Put your name and date at least. The information can be on the front or on a separate piece of fabric attached to the back.

REFERENCES

Encyclopedia of Ornament, The, by Albert Racinet

Japan's Cultural Heritage Reflected in the Star Lore of Orion, by Steve Renshaw and Saori Ihara, Oct. 1999 <http://www2.gol.com/users/stever/orion.htm> (accessed May 22, 2009.)

National Museum of American History, Smithsonian Institution, http://americanhistory.si.edu/collections/quilts/39.htm

Treasury of American Quilts, by Cyril I. Nelson and Carter Houck

For further information on these techniques, see the following books:
Appliqué:
Becky Goldsmith & Linda Jenkins Teach You to Appliqué the Piece O' Cake Way, by Becky Goldsmith & Linda Jenkins

Mastering Machine Appliqué, by Harriet Hargrave

The Quilters Ultimate Visual Guide, by Ellen Pahl

Machine Quilting:
Foolproof Machine Quilting, Mary Mashuta

Heirloom Machine Quilting, by Harriet Hargrave

Machine Quilting Made Easy, by Maurine Noble

Marci Baker

Recognized internationally for her expertise in quilting, Marci enjoys sharing ideas that simplify the process of quilting. A native of Dallas, Texas, Marci has loved sewing for years, making her first quilt at age 9 and sewing her own clothes in high school and college. She began teaching quilting in 1989 for her local quilting guild and shops. Marci graduated with a bachelors and master's degree in math. In 1993 she started Alicia's Attic with the concepts that combine her love of math with her love of quilting. Quilting became a great way to share her knowledge with others.

As an admirer of traditional quilts, Marci was inspired to author books on Not Your Grandmother's™ Quilts. This series uses the traditional patterns people associate with their grandmother and simplifies the technique. She has invented several tools to help make quilting easier for all. Her Know Before You Sew™ solution cards take common problems quilters encounter, and provide easy-to-understand solutions.

Marci spends much of the year traveling, teaching classes for quilting guilds and trade shows. Some of Marci's travels include Canada and Brazil. Enthusiasm and inspiration for quilting can be seen throughout her lectures, workshops, and books. She has been featured in Redbook, on Home and Garden TV's "Simply Quilts", Quilters' News Network, NBC's "The Jane Pauley Show", and has been published in numerous quilting magazines, including American Quilter Magazine.

In 2006 she expanded Alicia's Attic by purchasing Clearview Triangle from Sara Nephew. They are collaborating on new designs and techniques and have co-authored *Not Your Grandmother's Log Cabin.* These ideas and Marci's simplifying methods have come together as "The Clearview of Quilting", inspiring today's quilter.

Marci and her husband Clint, their sons Kevin and Marcus, and the family pet snake Scooby, currently live in Fort Collins, Colorado, near the mountains where they enjoy the beauty of life brought by nature's creation.

Contact her at marcibaker@aliciasattic.com.